How to Share
Your Faith
with
Anyone

TERRY BARBER

How to Share
Your Faith
with
Anyone

*A Practical Manual for
Catholic Evangelization*

IGNATIUS PRESS   SAN FRANCISCO

Cover photograph:
Bernini Columns, Saint Peter's Square, Vatican City
by Massimo Merlini/istockphoto.com

Cover design by Riz Boncan Marsella

© 2013 by Ignatius Press, San Francisco
All rights reserved
ISBN 978-1-58617-850-5
Library of Congress Control Number 2013940828
Printed in the United States of America ∞

DEDICATION

In gratitude for the many graces that I have received
through my baptism, through the Sacred Hearts of Jesus
and Mary, and through the protection of my guardian angel.

I hope this book will help you to fall in love with God.
As Saint Augustine says: "To fall in love with God is the
greatest of romances; to seek Him the greatest adventure;
to find Him the greatest human achievement."

I pray that this book will reach many souls
so that everyone can treasure the beauty of our
Faith and find the desire to share the Gospel.

"The New Evangelization that can make the twenty-first century a springtime of the Gospel is a task for the entire People of God, but will depend in a decisive way on the lay faithful being fully aware of their baptismal vocation and their responsibility for bringing the Good News of Jesus Christ to their culture and society."

—Blessed Pope John Paul II, 1998

CONTENTS

Foreword, by Scott Hahn 11

Introduction, by Matthew Arnold
"A Life of Evangelization" 15

Part One: What Is Evangelization?

1. Evangelization: It's Not Just for Protestants 33
2. What Is Evangelization? 37
3. Why Don't Catholics Evangelize? 41
4. Preparing for One-on-One Evangelization 45

Part Two: How to Evangelize

5. The Eight Laws of Effectively Sharing the Faith
   with Anyone 51
6. Jesus: The Perfect Evangelist 57
7. Planting Seeds for Jesus 63
8. The Ten Commandments of Evangelization 69
9. The Heart of Evangelization 87
10. How to Share Your Personal Testimony 93

Part Three: The Evangelist's Spiritual Game Plan

11. The Power of Prayer 105
12. Will Power 113

13. The Secret of Evangelization: Living
    in the Presence of God 119
14. Your Spiritual Game Plan 129
15. Evangelization "in the Margins" 135

Favorite Prayers and Reflections 147

Bibliography 153

FOREWORD

This book is more than you might think or hope it will be. It's not just another volume about apologetics. It's not another playbook full of strategies for winning arguments with your brother-in-law or coworkers. It's not a master plan for winning skirmishes in the culture wars.

It's a book about friendship. It's a book about love.

I know the title says it's about sharing the Faith, and the subtitle describes it as a practical manual, but sharing the Faith is a most refined expression of friendship and love—and love involves both deeds and words. Love involves a world of practicalities.

The traditional definition of *love* is to will the good of the other. We can wish no greater good for the people we know than that they live the Faith. The Faith is a gift we've received from God and want to share with all our friends. And the more we live the Faith, the more we want to share it; and so the Faith inspires us to make still more friends.

God created us for such a life. He created us for friendship. We are social beings, drawn to conversation and companionship. We prefer to work with other people who share our goals. We prefer to live in towns and neighborhoods. We mark our years off by times of celebration when we gather with others: birthday parties, holidays, vacations, and reunions. Friendship is a natural good that draws us to still higher goods. It draws us outside ourselves, toward others, so that we can share the goods we have, both material and spiritual. Friendship is all about a marvelous exchange, and the marvel is all the greater when we bring it to a supernatural level.

Friendship is the ordinary context for Christian witness in the world that God created. Terry Barber knows this, and so his manual is distinctively Catholic and different from some I knew when I was a young Protestant minister. Mr. Barber has written a manual that is practical, but he never leads us to turn people into projects or objects. People are meant to be friends, and friends are meant to be enriched by our gift of faith. Friendship, which is good by nature, can grow infinitely better by grace and can continue forever in heaven.

This book couldn't be more timely. Recent popes have, for decades, been calling the Church to a New Evangelization. In 1983 John Paul II announced that the New Evangelization was to be officially launched in 1992, because that would mark the five hundredth anniversary of the founding and first evangelization of the Americas. In preparation for that launch, he published an encyclical in 1990, *Redemptoris Missio*, and there he stated: "I sense that the moment has come to commit all of the Church's energies to a *New Evangelization*. . . . No believer in Christ, no institution of the Church, can avoid this supreme duty: to proclaim Christ to all peoples."

Note that there are no exemptions. Everybody is called to evangelize. Everybody is called to commit "all" energies and resources to this task.

Pope Benedict XVI, in turn, took up the theme with gusto, making it the focus of a world synod of bishops and a dominant motif in his Year of Faith. He clarified our mission. He stated frankly that we need to evangelize not only the people who have never heard of Christ, but also our neighbors who have been *de-Christianized*. It is sad that we can speak of many once-Christian people who have drifted from their baptismal commitment.

What's so new about the New Evangelization? First of all, it's to be carried out not just by missionaries, and not just by clergy, but by everyone. It's the job description of all the members of the Church. And, since most Catholics are laypeople, that means it will *primarily* be the work of laypeople—men and women, boys and girls, who witness to the Faith in the very ordinary circumstances of their workaday and school-day lives—in the context of their friendships.

But how? We laypeople don't preach like priests and deacons. Most of us don't teach like professors. How will we do it? That's what this book is all about: the nitty-gritty, practical, everyday, workplace, neighborhood, school, and home application of our universal call to "go out to all the world and tell the Good News".

The Church "exists", said Pope Paul VI, "in order to evangelize". Evangelization is the work of the whole Church. Evangelization is what we do—simply because we're Christian, simply because we're *Catholic*.

It's what we do, and it's who we are. If we don't evangelize, we simply *do not exist* as a Church; we simply *do not exist* as Christians.

Like Saint Paul, we are "compelled" to do this work. "Woe to me", he said, calling down a curse upon himself, "if I do not evangelize" (1 Cor 9:16).

But what blessings we'll know if we do. We'll know the blessing of fulfilling a mission we've been created to accomplish. We'll know the closeness of the Communion of Saints, even now! We'll know the joy of true friendship.

Scott Hahn, Ph.D.
Steubenville, Ohio
2013

INTRODUCTION

A LIFE OF EVANGELIZATION

I have always considered Terry Barber to be the "Sam Phillips of Catholic evangelization". At one time in the 1950s Phillips' recording label, Sun Records, had under contract Johnny Cash, Roy Orbison, Jerry Lee Lewis, Conway Twitty, and Elvis Presley. Each went on to be a huge star with multiple hit songs. Obviously, Phillips had an eye for talent. In a similar way, Terry Barber's Saint Joseph Communications has brought to national attention such prominent Catholic speakers as Jeff Cavins, Tim Staples, Steve Ray, Jesse Romero, Alex Jones, and Dr. Scott Hahn. To date Terry has produced and distributed over twenty million Catholic audio and video presentations. He has vigorously promoted several fledgling apostolates, such as Karl Keating's Catholic Answers, Patrick Madrid's *Envoy* magazine, Doug Barry's RADIX, and Father Juan Rivas' Hombre Nuevo, all of which have gone on to enjoy great success. More recently, he has launched Lighthouse Catholic Media, which has placed Catholic CDs in over six thousand parishes around the country so far. In many ways Terry Barber is the godfather of lay Catholic apologetics and evangelization in the United States.

You may know Terry from his popular Catholic radio shows, *Reasons for Faith LIVE* and *The Terry and Jesse Show*. Or you may be one of the thousands of people with whom

Terry has personally shared the Catholic Faith. Any way you slice it, Terry Barber is a remarkably successful Catholic evangelist. He has written this book to help you become one too. In a nutshell, here is his story.

Early Days

Born in 1956 and raised in the turbulent decades of the 1960s and '70s, Terry Barber did not go to Catholic school. Unlike many of his contemporaries, however, he also never bought into the "sex, drugs, and rock 'n' roll" mentality of the times. He credits this to being raised by two parents who really had the Catholic Faith. They brought him up on the *Baltimore Catechism*, which begins with a profound question about the meaning and purpose of life: "Why did God make you?" The answer: "To know, love, and serve God in this life and be happy with Him forever in the next." According to Terry this was a great advantage because he knew the basics: "I knew where I came from and where I'm going."

At age fourteen, Terry "fell in love with the Holy Mass". A man in his parish let young Terry borrow Archbishop Fulton J. Sheen's audio catechism, *Life Is Worth Living*. Terry was amazed at the way Sheen spoke and by the fact that one can be present at the once-and-for-all, eternal sacrifice of Calvary every day at Holy Mass. He was hooked for life and has been a daily communicant ever since.

From this point Terry began to study the mysteries of the Faith more deeply, but he was not "all work and no play". Sports, especially baseball, were also very important in his life. As a high school senior in 1975 he was All-League and batting champ at Covina High. "That was my life: my faith and my sports."

After high school, Terry tried out for the Oakland A's but did not make the cut. With his heart set on a career in baseball, he trained to be a professional umpire. He was certified for Triple-A ball but quickly became disillusioned by the worldly realities of professional sports. Seeking a way of life more in line with his Catholic convictions, he took classes in apologetics, Christology, Mariology, and the documents of Vatican II from the Knights of the Immaculata in the summer of 1978. From there he volunteered at the Franciscan friary of Marytown in Kenosha, Wisconsin, to discern whether he had a vocation to the religious life.

During his stay with the Franciscans, it was discovered that someone was stealing gasoline from the brothers' private pump. Ever helpful, Terry staked out the gas pump to catch the culprits red-handed. One night his patience was rewarded, and he drove off the would-be thieves with a baseball bat! The Franciscans told Terry that he was probably not cut out for the religious life.

On the advice of a friend, Terry decided to try real estate. He was trained in the "seven basic laws of selling" by sales guru Al Tomsik. He then attended a career seminar with twelve hundred other prospective realtors. Famous broker Bruce Mulhearn asked the audience, "Who can sell me this pencil?" Terry responded using Tomsik's basic laws of selling to show the benefits of owning a pencil. Mulhearn said, "Young man, I want to take you to lunch. You're going to make it in this business."

It was then that Terry realized the power of these sales techniques. Based on timeless principles of human nature, they became—when combined with the truths of divine revelation—the foundation of his effective style of evangelization. As Terry says, "I used to sell real estate on planet earth; now I sell real estate in heaven."

Employing the basic laws of selling made Terry one of Red Carpet Realty's top twenty Southern California realtors by 1982. Young and successful, he remained a daily communicant and looked for opportunities to fulfill the call of Vatican II to "sanctify the secular order" as a layperson. In 1978 he founded Saint Joseph Communications, a Catholic audio tape ministry. What was his first project? Bishop Sheen's *Life Is Worth Living*.

Lay Apostolate

In 1978, Terry wrote to Archbishop Sheen at the Society for the Propagation of the Faith to ask permission to copy and to sell the original audio series of *Life Is Worth Living* on cassette. Once he had permission, Terry borrowed a copy of the series on LP phonograph records from a local priest and transferred them to cassette in his mother's living room.

In February 1979 he took his *Life Is Worth Living* tapes to the Los Angeles Archdiocese's Religious Education Congress —the largest meeting of this sort in the country. While he was there a priest told him, "You're wasting your time. Bishop Sheen is antiquated. His teachings were good back then, but they are useless today." Terry was polite, but took the remark as a personal challenge. He purchased a full-page ad for his newly formed Saint Joseph Communications (SJC) in the Catholic newspaper *Our Sunday Visitor*. The response was tremendous, and *Our Sunday Visitor* presented SJC a top-advertiser award. Catholic books on tape and recorded presentations from other speakers soon followed.

December 9, 1979, saw the death of the great Catholic communicator Fulton J. Sheen. In the hope of attending the archbishop's funeral Mass, Terry waited at the airport for a standby flight to New York and put the outcome in God's hands. He got on the last flight of the day, the red-eye from LA to New York, and arrived in time to attend the viewing of Sheen's coffin.

A TV reporter spotted Terry carrying his little suitcase. Inquiring where Terry was from, the reporter put him on camera and asked, "Why would a young person like you come all the way from Los Angeles to attend Bishop Sheen's funeral?"

Terry's uncle Charlie in Scranton, Pennsylvania, watched his nephew's response on TV: "Because Bishop Sheen taught me the meaning and purpose of life; his material needs to go back on radio and television because the world is in desperate need of knowing the meaning and purpose of life, and Bishop Sheen gave them that. That's why I'm here."

At the funeral Terry spoke with dozens of people about how Bishop Sheen had affected their lives. He was more determined than ever to get Sheen's teaching out to the world.

Like Father, Like Son

In 1985 Terry's dad, Harry Barber, took seriously ill with shrinking of the brain, and Terry moved back home to help his folks. Terry had helped his mom and dad through the terminal illness of his brother Richard, who had succumbed to brain cancer in 1977. Now, in his remaining five years, Harry was in and out of the VA hospital twenty-six times for various operations.

During one stay, Terry's dad shared a room with a man who had been out of the Church for thirty years. Harry suggested that they go downstairs to the hospital's Mass. "We'll go early, and you can go to confession first." The man did. A year later, he looked Harry up and came to visit. By that time the man was a volunteer at his parish and a daily communicant, and he wanted to thank Harry for the invitation that had brought him back to Christ and His Church. You can see why Terry comes by his love of evangelization naturally.

To make living with his folks easier on them, Terry built a little apartment for himself off his mom and dad's garage. That garage became the duplication center of Saint Joseph Communications, which was now Terry's full-time apostolate. One day a woman at the VA hospital warned Terry that he was wasting his life caring for his now-bedridden father at home and that Harry should be institutionalized. As usual, Terry used this as an opportunity for evangelization and explained the Catholic understanding of the value of suffering.

Terry brought his dad Holy Communion each day, and Harry offered his suffering for the apostolate. Harry's example of humility and redemptive suffering was a powerful experience for his son. "My dad showed me resignation to God's will", says Terry.

On July 12, 1989—his forty-second wedding anniversary —Harry Barber passed into eternity. Terry recalls, "My mom and dad had the day together; he was conscious. It was a gift from God.''

Terry's mom also understood the value of sacrifice and suffering. Vera Barber was a great help to the apostolate. Affectionately known as ''Grandma'' she volunteered for Saint Joe's for two dozen years—editing, shipping, doing whatever was needed. Terry says she could ''clam'' (package a CD in a plastic shell) over twenty-five thousand CDs in a month—nearly a thousand a day! ''That's the kind of zeal my mother had for souls.'' Even in her final illness she would clam CDs in her bed, by that time an ordeal of several painful minutes for each one. In 2008 she died surrounded by her children and grandchildren with Terry holding one hand and his brother Patrick holding the other.

From seeing to their children's religious education in the turbulent sixties to offering their time and effort to the lay apostolate, Terry's parents set a good example that has stayed with him for life.

Wedding Bells

In 1989, Terry married Mary Danielle Doyle. Terry is thankful that his dad got to meet her before he died.

Terry first met ''Danielle'' on a Mission Immaculata retreat in Rosemead, California, in 1978. Ten years later, in October 1988, they met again, at Holy Mass. Danielle, a schoolteacher, was spending a year volunteering for the Knights of the Immaculata in Terry's hometown of Covina. She shared an apartment with two friends right across from his parish church.

One day Terry asked Danielle and her roommates if they would like to join his Shield of Roses group to pray the Holy Rosary outside a local abortion clinic. They all said yes, but when he came to pick them up, only Danielle was there. Her two roommates were discerning a vocation to the religious life as Carmelite nuns. He didn't know it, but he was being set up.

Terry and Danielle were the first to arrive at the abortion clinic. They were surprised by the presence of 150 pro-abortion activists from the National Organization for Women (NOW). As soon as Terry and Danielle stepped out of the car, the NOW group yelled, "There they are!" The pro-abortion agitators said they believed that Operation Rescue was going to block the entrance of the clinic and had come to prevent that.

Terry told Danielle, "Don't worry. I don't know what they're here for, but we're just here to pray the Rosary." Although the rest of their group had not arrived, Terry and Daniel started to pray. The NOW group surrounded them, shouting blasphemies and hurling threats and insults. One man snuck up behind Terry to shove a lit cigarette butt in his ear. Terry recalls, "My lower nature kicked in, and I went after the guy, but he disappeared into the crowd." No longer able to pray with the same concentration as before, Terry decided to prepare himself for any other assaults; he would be ready with "a proportionate response".

All the local TV stations—including the network affiliates—were there to interview the pro-abortion group who claimed they were protecting the clinic from "anti-abortion terrorists". Terry approached a KTLA-TV reporter and asked if she were interested in hearing the other side of the story, "or is this going to be all one-sided?"

She asked, "What organization are you with?"

Thinking quickly, Terry invented the organization Coalition of Concerned Roman Catholics of America and identified himself as the president. With an official identity he was able to go on TV to explain what they were really doing there.

When the interview aired, the commentator reported that the National Organization for Women had come to stop an Operation Rescue "attack" on the clinic, but that all they found was a handful of Roman Catholics praying the Rosary for aborted babies and offering women alternatives to abortion. As Terry says, "She got it."

But for Terry the story does not end there. Throughout the ordeal Danielle kept praying the Rosary, eyes closed. When they got in the car to leave, Terry said, "I'm sure glad that's over. But what I want to know is how did you keep praying? Weren't you scared?"

She replied, "I was at first. But once I asked my guardian angel for protection, I was able to pray."

Terry replied, "Hey, if I poke you with a pin, will you bleed? I want to take you out to dinner to find out a little more about you."

The rest, as they say, is history. Terry and Mary Danielle were married on October 7, 1989, the feast of the Most Holy Rosary. They honeymooned in Fatima.

In November of 1989, after the happy couple had returned to the states, Karl Keating told Terry that a former Protestant minister was giving his conversion testimony at a parish in Riverside, California. There was no one else available to record the event, so Terry went himself. That was how he met Dr. Scott Hahn.

A Protestant Minister Becomes Catholic

In his book *Rome Sweet Home*, Scott Hahn describes his first meeting with Terry Barber:

> The talk was similar to one I had given a dozen times before; but this time it turned out to be different than any other. It was to become "The Tape" (otherwise known as *A Protestant Minister Becomes Catholic*).
>
> Ten minutes before I started, I was introduced to Terry Barber of Saint Joseph Communications, who was hastily assembling some tape-recording equipment for my talk. As he set up the microphone, he explained to me how he and his brand-new bride, Danielle, had just arrived back home from their honeymoon in Fatima, Portugal. He also explained his lateness; he had recorded talks at five separate locations that day. Terry made it seem it was a last-minute decision even to show up at my talk. At the time, it didn't really matter to me; later on, we were both eternally grateful.
>
> At 7:30 sharp, I was introduced to a small group of thirty-five people. After talking for over an hour—I have never ended anything on time—I took a short break and got back up for the Q&A session. When it was all over, I walked toward the back to talk with Pat [Madrid].

While we were talking, Terry Barber came running up waving a copy of a cassette tape. "God is going to use this tape, my friend, I just know it."

I was pleased to see him so excited, but since I had given the same talk on so many occasions when it had been taped, I did not think anything of it. I even thought to myself: How unprepared I was tonight; other times it was much better. Maybe that's why our Lord chose to use this particular talk in such a powerful way—since no one could take any of the credit but Him. [. . .]

A few weeks passed before I heard again from Terry Barber. He phoned to tell me he had been sending out dozens of free copies of the tape to various Catholic leaders and groups across the country. Terry reported that he was getting a wonderful response.

Little did I know; the tape would change both our lives. [. . .]

"No wonder," I said. "What would you expect from such entrepreneurial effort? Terry, I think you have the determination of an apostle."

For his part, Terry considered Scott a modern-day Fulton Sheen, in terms of his ability to communicate the truths of the Faith effectively. At that first meeting Scott agreed to record fifty more talks for Saint Joseph Communications. A handshake was the only contract. From that meeting came *Growth by Oath*, *Answering Common Objections*, *Salvation History*, *The Lamb's Supper*, *The Fourth Cup*, and a litany of powerful series produced by Saint Joseph Communications.

But it all started with Scott's conversion tape. It became the most widely distributed Catholic audiotape of all time.

Mark Brumley, president of Ignatius Press, said, "What Terry Barber did was brilliant. By giving away that tape he built a demand for Scott Hahn's material that would never have existed without that introduction."

Untold thousands of souls were touched by Scott's conversion testimony, and many Protestants came into the Church, including some two hundred Protestant ministers. Many of them had to abandon their livelihoods to enter the Church. With Scott's help, one such minister, Marcus Grodi, started the Coming Home Network, an apostolate dedicated to helping Protestant ministers deal with the many repercussions of becoming Catholic. Terry likened these conversions to a new Oxford Movement. Not since the conversion of the Anglican John Henry Cardinal Newman in the nineteenth century had the testimony of one man brought so many Protestant clergy into the Church.

But along with the conversions, many cradle Catholics also began to study their Faith seriously because of Dr. Hahn's presentations. As Terry knew all too well, the plain fact is that the generation of Catholics who grew up after Vatican II was so poorly catechized that they really did not know the fundamentals of their own religion. Terry seized the moment to step in and fill that void. Bishop Sheen and Dr. Scott Hahn were a powerful one-two punch for thousands upon thousands of Catholics who were inspired to learn more about their Faith. Scott Hahn went on to be a best-selling author, a celebrated Catholic theologian, and one of the most popular Catholic speakers in the world. Almost a quarter of a century later, Saint Joseph Communications and Dr. Hahn's Saint Paul Center for Biblical Theology still cosponsor the annual West Coast Biblical Studies Conference each January in Riverside, California.

The Catholic Family Conference

In 1990 Scott spoke at Saint Cyprian's Church in Long Beach. That day-long conference spawned an annual event dubbed the National Catholic Family Conference. In 1996 Terry founded a nonprofit organization called the Catholic Resource Center (CRC) so that Catholics could donate to the many works of evangelization that had begun through the conference.

The National Catholic Family Conference soon outgrew Saint Cyprian's and moved to the Long Beach Convention Center. By 1999 the conference was attracting as many as 7,500 Catholics from all over the country. The conference featured Holy Mass, confessions, and talks from many of the finest Catholic speakers in the nation. All weekend there were continuous presentations in the main room, plus two simultaneous breakout sessions, as well as full programs for teens and children. It was a colossal undertaking and eventually outgrew the facilities at Long Beach. In the year 2000 the conference moved again, this time to the Anaheim Convention Center near Disneyland. Today the Family Conference tradition continues in California at the Ontario Convention Center. Since 1999 a Midwest Catholic Family Conference has been held in Wichita, Kansas.

Over the years the Catholic Resource Center has branched out into many other activities, primarily concerned with evangelization. The CRC has distributed tens of thousands of tapes, videos, books, CDs, and DVDs about the Catholic Faith around the country and around the world. In one of its costliest efforts, in 2003 the Resource Center saved a beautiful century-old traditional Catholic Church from the wrecking ball. The Sacred Heart Chapel in Covina is now headquarters for CRC and SJC and is available for weddings and other events. It is also the home of a Melkite Catholic community, as well as regular Bible studies and several weekend conferences each year. But among the CRC's many activities, perhaps their most powerful method of sharing the Faith has been Catholic radio.

Catholic Radio

The year 1985 saw the birth of Saint Joseph Radio. Terry bought thirty minutes of airtime on a local radio station, KPLS. Naturally, his first broadcast was a recording of Archbishop Fulton J. Sheen. The show included Saint Joe's phone number so that listeners could call to order the tape. Their first phone call came from a man who had been away from the Church for over twenty-five years. The broadcast had inspired him to return to the practice of the Faith, he said. Terry remembers, "That first half hour cost us $300. I have been involved in Catholic radio ever since, but if we had done no more radio after that first show, it would have been worth it." Sheen's *Life Is Worth Living* is still being played on Catholic radio today.

In 1998 the Catholic Resource Center began broadcasting locally in Southern California. I was brought in to produce two Monday-through-Friday programs, *Saint Joseph's Journal* and *The Splendor of Truth*. In 1999 they went on the air around the world via EWTN's Global Catholic Radio Network. CRC's first live program was *Reasons for Faith LIVE* with original host Tim Staples. That was soon followed by *Scripture Matters LIVE with Dr. Scott Hahn*, which Terry was pleased to produce and to host from 1999 to 2002. The CRC is still producing live radio for EWTN and Immaculate Heart Radio.

Evangelization Today

In 2005 Terry founded Lighthouse Catholic Media with Mark Middendorf and Dave Durand. The inspiration for the program was to provide CDs to parishes, where those who need them most can have easy access to them. Through this program, Lighthouse sets up in the back of a parish church an attractive kiosk with CDs and brochures on the Catholic Faith available for a small donation. It has been a resounding success. Terry himself placed the first Lighthouse kiosk in February of 2005. In 2012 Lighthouse CDs were available in over six thousand churches, with one-third of U.S. parishes participating in the program. Lighthouse also has over eighteen thousand subscribers to their CD of the Month Club. They distribute over 1.5 million CDs each year—and they are just getting started.

God has blessed Terry Barber with many opportunities for evangelization. Today, along with serving on the board of Lighthouse Catholic Media, he remains president of Saint Joseph Communications and the Catholic Resource Center, distributing Catholic CDs and DVDs and promoting live events. He is also a popular Catholic radio personality with *The Terry and Jesse Show* on Immaculate Heart Radio and is the cohost of the long-running *Reasons for Faith LIVE* on the EWTN Global Catholic Radio Network. Through the CRC's radio ministry he and Jesse Romero are evangelizing thousands each week.

Through the years, Terry Barber's every effort at promoting Catholic CDs and DVDs, books, radio shows, live conferences, and so forth have had one goal: to "multiply" himself and to equip an army of on-fire evangelists to fight in the battle for souls. That is why Terry personally trains

Lighthouse Catholic Media's more than five hundred representatives in how to promote the Faith through the program. He calls his method the Eight Laws of Effectively Sharing the Faith with Anyone. The Lighthouse representatives are blessed to learn from Terry how to use these timeless principles for the purpose of evangelization. Now it is your turn.

Terry Barber could have produced an encyclopedia of evangelization just from his many notebooks full of quotes from Scripture, the Magisterium, and the Fathers, saints, and Doctors of the Church. But that is not what he wanted; as he often asserts, "I'm not a theologian; I'm Joe Six-Pack." Instead he has distilled the essence of his thirty years of sharing the Catholic Faith into a concise manual for practical evangelization filled with examples from his own life. What you hold in your hands is a roadmap for lay Catholics to spread the Gospel of Jesus Christ effectively in the modern world. The techniques presented in this little book will empower you to share with family, friends, and even strangers the truths Jesus entrusted to His Holy Catholic Church. But it will also help you to grow closer to our Lord and enable you to say with Terry's beloved "spiritual friend" Venerable Fulton J. Sheen, "Any good we do comes from God, and we thank Him for it."

Matthew Arnold
Garden Grove, California
2013

PART ONE

WHAT IS EVANGELIZATION?

I

EVANGELIZATION:
IT'S NOT JUST FOR PROTESTANTS

God has created me to do Him some definite service;
He has committed some work to me which He has
not committed to another. I have my mission.

— Blessed John Henry Cardinal Newman

I think most people associate evangelization with Fundamentalist Christians and pseudo-Christian groups such as
the Jehovah's Witnesses. But according to the teaching of
Vatican II, it is the main duty of Catholic men and women
to "bear witness to Christ" in our lives and in our works.
In our home, on the job, in our social group or professional
circle, we must show forth "the new man created according
to God in justice and true holiness". The Gospel of Jesus
Christ must be proclaimed by what we say and do. This is
evangelization.

Now, I did not make this up. This is the official teaching
of the Second Vatican Council. But if you are like 99 percent
of Catholics, you have probably never read the documents
of Vatican II. That is why I am "preaching to the choir" in
this book—because, in plain language, lay Catholics need
to know that we are on the earth precisely to sanctify secular society. We have a duty to give our family, our friends,

and our neighbors—and that means everybody—the Good News of Jesus Christ.

In the 1960s Pope Paul VI taught that the "pressing need to evangelize the multitudes" through mass media is no excuse to abandon one-on-one evangelization. Our gift of faith is an inheritance from God that is meant to be shared with a lost and hurting society. But the late pontiff also reminds us that one-on-one evangelization is never an "isolated act" because evangelization is a "deeply ecclesial" activity. Therefore individual Catholic communities have the task of learning the essence of the Gospel message and sharing it.

What Pope Paul VI was telling us is that there is no place for "Lone Ranger-ism" in the work of evangelization. Simply put, "Jesus and me" Christianity is absolutely alien to Holy Scripture and Sacred Tradition. As lay Catholics—even when we evangelize as individuals—we really evangelize through, with, and in the Church.

Evangelization is a mandate for all the lay faithful, but it must take place in communion with our pastors—the priests and bishops Jesus gives to His Church—and with the Magisterium (the Church's official teaching office of the Pope and the bishops under him). Likewise, the growth of the Church is the "consolation of the Holy Spirit". The Holy Spirit is the "soul of the Church" and the main source of all Catholic ministry.

There is a profound link between Christ, the Church, and evangelization. It is vital that your local parish reflect and express true unity with Holy Mother Church, because the more your local church is attached to the universal Church—especially in being faithful to the Magisterium—the "more it will be truly evangelizing". Union between the local Church and the universal Church is essential because all Catholic Christians need to be on the same page; centered on the Holy Eucharist, devoted to Mary, faithful to our Holy Father, the Pope, and sharing the one, holy, catholic, and apostolic Faith.

Light from the Word

Evangelization is a duty

"Woe to me if I do not preach the Gospel" (1 Cor 9:16).

Have confidence

"Do not be afraid; just have faith" (Mk 5:36).

Evangelization must be done "through and with" the Church

"You are a chosen race, a royal priesthood, a holy nation, God's own people, that you may declare the wonderful deeds of him who called you out of darkness into his marvelous light" (1 Pet 2:9, RSV).

"To bring to light [for all] what is the plan of the mystery hidden from ages past in God . . . so that the manifold wisdom of God might now be made known through the church" (Eph 3:9–10).

Union with priests and bishops is crucial

"Obey your leaders and submit to them; for they are keeping watch over your souls, as men who will have to give account" (Heb 13:17, RSV).

2

WHAT IS EVANGELIZATION?

The word *evangelization* comes from the Greek word *euange-lion*. It originally came into English as *gospel*, which literally means "good news". To evangelize simply means to share the Gospel, the Good News of Jesus Christ. This is the first and most fundamental element of evangelization.

So here is the next logical question: What is the Good News? The Good News is the answer to the deep questions of life: Why are we here? Is this world all there is? What is the meaning and purpose of life?

God created human beings in order that we might have a personal relationship with Him now and forever. But most do not enjoy this relationship because it has been broken by sin: the sin of our first parents—which we all inherit when we come into this world—and the sins we have personally committed in what we have done and in what we have failed to do. Some of the consequences of sin are fear, loneliness, emptiness, and guilt—but the worst consequence is eternal separation from God. There is nothing that human beings can do to bridge the gap between God and man caused by sin. That is the bad news.

But the Good News is that through the Paschal Mystery—the life, death, and Resurrection of Jesus Christ—salvation from sin is available to everyone as a gift of God's grace and mercy. The sacrifice of the sinless God-man on the Cross was one of atonement and satisfaction for our sins. In other words, Jesus paid a debt He did not owe because we owed a debt we could not pay.

> If our greatest need had been information, God would have sent us an educator. If our greatest need had been technology, God would have sent us a scientist. If our greatest need had been money, God would have sent us an economist. If our greatest need had been pleasure, God would have sent us an entertainer. But our greatest need was forgiveness of sins, so God sent us a Savior. Jesus Christ is the source and summit of our life. (Venerable Fulton J. Sheen)

Through Christ, eternity has entered human life. Now, human life is called to make the journey with Christ from time to eternity. To this end, Jesus founded a Church that mediates His grace and mercy to the world through the sacraments that He instituted.

Light from the Word

Sin is the problem, and Jesus is the solution

> "For the wages of sin is death, but the gift of God is eternal life in Christ Jesus our Lord" (Rom 6:23).

> "For God so loved the world that he gave his only Son, so that everyone who believes in him might not perish but might have eternal life" (Jn 3:16).

Only Jesus can heal our broken relationship with God

> "I am the way and the truth and the life. No one comes to the Father except through me" (Jn 14:6).

"There is no salvation in anyone else, for there is no other name in the whole world given to men by which we are to be saved." (Acts 4:12, RSV).

Jesus founded a Church to continue His saving mission

"And so I say to you, you are Peter, and upon this rock I will build my church, and the gates of the netherworld shall not prevail against it" (Mt 16:18).

"Whoever listens to you listens to me. Whoever rejects you rejects me. And whoever rejects me rejects the one who sent me" (Lk 10:16).

"Go, therefore, and make disciples of all nations, baptizing them in the name of the Father, and of the Son, and of the Holy Spirit, teaching them to observe all that I have commanded you. And behold, I am with you always, until the end of the age" (Mt 28:19−20).

3

WHY DON'T CATHOLICS EVANGELIZE?

I hope it is clear beyond the shadow of a doubt that all Catholics—and that means you—have been given a mandate by Sacred Scripture and the Magisterium of the Church to share their Catholic Faith with others. So why don't more Catholics evangelize? I suspect the main reason is fear. You can have a conversation about religious leaders such as Buddha or Muhammad without fear, but not about Jesus. Why? Because Jesus claimed to be God, and this makes people uncomfortable; sometimes even hostile. We live in a pluralistic and secular society in which Jesus' exclusive claim, "I am the way and the truth and the life. No one comes to the Father except through me" (Jn 14:6) is considered intolerant.

Yet in our modern secular culture the media (radio, TV, movies, the Internet) daily heap ridicule on Christians in general and on the Catholic Church in particular. This is a not-so-subtle form of genuine intolerance and, dare I say it, persecution. Let's face it: if the kinds of things that are regularly said about Catholics were directed at any other religion or group, those remarks would be roundly condemned as downright bigoted; yet anti-Catholicism gets a free pass. This might be hypocrisy, but that's the current reality. Since no one likes to be mocked, fear of ridicule is one reason

Catholics don't evangelize. Also, some Catholics fear that sharing the Gospel may get them branded a fundamentalist or a religious fanatic and cause them to lose the respect of their friends.

Another fear that keeps some Catholics from evangelizing is that of being humiliated because they are unable to explain adequately the doctrines of the Church. These Catholics fear that they do not know the Scriptures as well as their Bible-quoting or that they cannot make a logical, reasoned defense that will satisfy an unbeliever. Simply put, they are afraid that their answers will not be good enough. For some this is only the fear of embarrassment and strained relations; for others it is the fear that their less-than-perfect efforts at evangelization may turn people off altogether.

Still other Catholics are simply apathetic. "I have my religion, and I'm happy with it. That's good enough for me. I don't need to push it on anybody else." Considering the mandate of Scripture and the Church outlined in the previous chapters, this is the weakest excuse of all.

What lay Catholics need to remember is that what we are sharing really is Good News and the world needs to hear it. Many lost and broken people long to hear the Gospel and don't even know it. And many non-Catholic Christians are amazed to learn that Catholicism is actually much more Biblical than their Evangelical Protestant or Fundamentalist denomination.

Also, most opportunities for evangelization are only a matter of "planting seeds", as our Lord told us in the parable of the sower (Mt 13:1–23; Mk 4:3–20; Lk 8:4–18). In the following chapters you will find the information you need to overcome anxieties about evangelizing and, I hope, be inspired to move beyond fear or apathy and to share your Catholic Faith with a hurting world that acts as if God does not exist.

4

PREPARING FOR
ONE-ON-ONE EVANGELIZATION

The whole Church is missionary and the work of
evangelization [is] the fundamental task of the people of God.

—Vatican II, *Decree on the
Missionary Activity of the Church*

The late Father John Hardon, S.J., was a holy priest, a great
Catholic evangelist, and the founder of the Marian Cate-
chists. He once said to me, "Terry, I can honestly tell you
that the future of the Church in our country depends heav-
ily on the zeal of lay Catholics like you." The fact is, all the
baptized, not just clergy and religious, are enlisted to evangelize. We are on a mission from God and His missionary
Church. The Vatican II *Decree on the Apostolate of Lay People*
(no. 2) puts it this way:

> In the Church, there is diversity of services but unity of
> purpose. Christ conferred on the apostles and their suc-
> cessors the duty of teaching, sanctifying, and ruling in His
> name and power. But the laity, too, share in the priestly,
> prophetic, and royal office of Christ and therefore have
> their own role to play in the mission of the whole people
> of God in the Church and in the world. They exercise a
> genuine apostolate by their activity on behalf of bringing
> the gospel and holiness to men, and on behalf of penetrating
> and perfecting the temporal sphere of things through the

spirit of the gospel. In this way, their temporal activity can openly bear witness to Christ and promote the salvation of men. Since it is proper to the layman's state in life for him to spend his days in the midst of the world and of secular transactions, he is called by God to burn with the spirit of Christ and to exercise his apostolate in the world as a kind of leaven.

All of us are called to be missionaries, first in our homes, and then in the secular world of work, school, social groups, and so forth. Although I do not belong to Opus Dei, I love its spirituality of laypeople finding their mission in the ordinary activities of life.

I share with you here what I have shared again and again with Catholics all over the country, on radio and in person: The key to sharing your faith is living always in the presence of God. In the first place this means living a sacramental life of frequent Communion and regular confession. You must also have an active prayer life. Being aware of God's presence in your life means you will always be asking, "Lord, what do YOU want me to do in this situation?" And I must tell you that living in the presence of God is essential in order to practice virtue and to keep away from sin.

The Catholic Church needs laypeople who want to live in the presence of God, who know the truths of the Faith, and who are willing and able to share them with others. I often tell the story of a five-year-old boy I met at a conference. He tugged on my pants leg and asked, "Hey, mister, do you know who made you?"

"Yes."

"Who?"

I answered, "God made me."

"That's right," he beamed, "and God made me, too!"

This little fellow had just learned the answer to his first catechism question and was already sharing it with others! The point is the 99 percent of the Church that is laypeople all need to be like that little boy: ready, willing, and able to share our Faith.

But where do you begin? There are many avenues of evangelization—for example, CDs, pamphlets, websites, and Catholic radio—but there is no substitute for personal contact. One-on-one evangelization is very powerful. The Lord will give you opportunities to evangelize according to your state in life. They could be at home, in the workplace, on the soccer field, or in line at the grocery store. Do not forsake these opportunities!

Now, you might think, "But, Terry, I don't know what to say!" That is why you are reading this book! You can become an effective evangelist with the help of the Holy Spirit and with proper preparation.

The *Decree on the Apostolate of Lay People* (no. 28) teaches that training is necessary for effective evangelization. This training includes both your continual spiritual and doctrinal progress and the development of your ability to adapt your faith-sharing to various circumstances. Jesus Himself was able to talk to friends, adversaries, common people, government officials, and religious leaders alike. And as you read the Gospels you will discover that He evangelized not only in synagogues and in the Temple, but anywhere the opportunity arose: in a fishing boat, at a dinner party, on a hillside, beside a well, and so on. He showed us the way, and now He calls us to follow His example.

Light from the Word

We are called to mission

"We are ambassadors for Christ" (2 Cor 5:20).

Unity is crucial

"[There will be] one Lord, one faith, one baptism" (Eph 4:5).

"Behold, how good and pleasant it is when brothers dwell in unity" (Ps 133:1, RSV).

Preparation is necessary

"Do your best to present yourself to God as one approved, a workman who has no need to be ashamed, rightly handling the word of truth" (2 Tim 2:15, RSV).

Follow the example of Jesus

"Take my yoke upon you and learn from me" (Mt 11:29a).

"If anyone wishes to come after me, he must deny himself and take up his cross daily and follow me" (Lk 9:23).

PART TWO

HOW TO EVANGELIZE

5

THE EIGHT LAWS OF EFFECTIVELY
SHARING THE FAITH WITH ANYONE

When I present my evangelization course at parishes, I always begin each session by reviewing what I call the Eight Laws of Effectively Sharing the Faith with Anyone:

1. Keep it simple.
2. Keep him saying yes.
3. Be enthusiastic.
4. Call him by name.
5. Show and then tell.
6. Always agree.
7. Ask questions.
8. Practice virtue.

These laws are based on the immutable principles of selling that I learned in my real-estate days and are invaluable for effective evangelization. I have used them successfully in Catholic radio ministry and one-on-one evangelization for over thirty years in an effort to follow the mandate of the Second Vatican Council by helping as many people as I can to fall in love with Christ and His Church. Let's look at each law to see how it applies to sharing the Faith.

1. Keep It Simple

You should not get too complicated when you are teaching someone to fall in love with God; that is, do not try to share too much, because people can absorb only a limited amount of information at a time. This is especially true if what you are sharing is new to them. Also, try not to be too "theological" or to get into heavy philosophy when you are sharing your Faith. Presenting the Gospel simply and with genuine concern for others is much more fruitful.

2. Keep Him Saying Yes

Establishing common ground is very important when sharing the Faith. A powerful way to do this is by asking questions or making statements with which the other person will naturally agree. For example, when speaking with a Bible-believing Christian you might say, "We both believe the Bible is the inspired word of God, right? Well, look what Jesus says about the Eucharist in John 6:22–59." You might also say, "We both know that the word *pope* is not in the Bible", with which he will readily agree, but then show him Matthew 16:13–20 or John 21:15–17 to show how Jesus clearly makes Peter the earthly head of His Church.

Even if the person you are sharing your Faith with is an agnostic, you might ask, "If there is an afterlife, wouldn't it be better to go to heaven than to go to hell?" Any sane person would answer yes to that, even if only in his heart.

3. Be Enthusiastic

Genuine enthusiasm is crucial to effective evangelization. The Greek word *theos*, meaning "God", is the root of the word *enthusiasm*, which literally means "being in God". The presence of God shows forth in your attitude. Even something as simple as a smile is a small form of enthusiasm. If you smile when you share the Gospel, I guarantee you will be a more effective evangelist. When you share the Good News, you are giving someone a priceless gift from God Himself! If you can't get enthusiastic about that, maybe you had better check your pulse!

4. Call Him by Name

Always ask for the name of the person with whom you are sharing the Faith. Using a person's name is powerful; he cannot help but respond to his name. Using a person's name in conversation is a proven way to keep his attention and to make what you are sharing more significant to him personally.

5. Show and Then Tell

Rather than just telling someone about the beauty of the Eucharist, why not show it to him? For example, you might take him to an adoration chapel. I know that many people have been converted in the presence of our Lord in the Blessed Sacrament. Experiencing the reality of God's presence is more convincing than hearing someone talk about it.

Here is another example of "show and then tell". In a conversation with a Bible-believing Christian, rather than telling him that a particular Catholic doctrine is biblical, show him the doctrine in the Scriptures and have him read it for himself. It is said that 88 percent of everything we learn comes through the eyes, so remember the old saying: "Seeing is believing."

6. Always Agree

In the Gospel of Saint Matthew Jesus says, "Agree quickly with your adversary" (Mt 5:25, KJV). This does not mean that you should water down your message. You should, however, remain positive and not argue with anyone.

"But, Terry," you might ask, "what if someone is arguing with me?" In that situation, call him by name and ask a question: "So-and-so, am I correct that what you are saying is . . . ?" and then summarize his point. This is not agreeing in the sense of accepting what the person is saying, but rather in the sense of showing that you understand what he is saying.

7. Ask Questions

If I were to ask you what color car you drive, even if you do not tell me, the answer is in your mind. That is why salesmen are taught this saying: "He who asks questions has control." In other words, by asking questions, you can keep someone's attention and steer it in a particular direction. By asking a lot of questions, the Greek philosopher Socrates not only led the conversation, but also helped his listeners to discover the truth. When I evangelize I constantly ask questions. As you can see from the examples given earlier, asking questions is a key ingredient for successful evangelization. Often the way to bring people to Christ and His Church is not by telling them anything at all, but by asking them the right questions.

8. Practice Virtue

You should practice virtue at all times, but especially when you are sharing the Faith. Let's face it: if you are not "walking the talk", people could not care less what you say. Jesus says, "This is how all will know that you are my disciples, if you have love for one another" (Jn 13:35). So, it is by the way you live your life—the good example you set at home, at work, at school, and in social settings—that others will know that you really follow Jesus Christ. Remember the old axiom: "People don't care how much you know until they know how much you care."

The Four Stages of Evangelization

Now that you know the Eight Laws of Effectively Sharing the Faith with Anyone, I should also tell you that every effective faith-sharing encounter is made up of four distinct stages. You must lead the person you are evangelizing through the following stages if he is to come to a decision:

1. Attention
2. Interest
3. Decision
4. Action

How do you get the person's attention? Keep it simple, and call him by name. How do you hold his interest? Ask questions; keep him saying yes; show and then tell. How do you encourage his desire for the Gospel? Always agree; be enthusiastic; practice virtue. After these three steps, action follows. What this action might be depends on the encounter. With an Evangelical Christian, perhaps you can share a moment of prayer or set a time to talk again. To an unbaptized person you might suggest looking into the RCIA program at his local parish. You might invite a fallen-away Catholic to go to confession and Communion.

I train sales representatives for Lighthouse Catholic Media, and when I share with them the Eight Laws and the Four Stages I tell them, "If you want to see the true worth of these principles, try them with your own kids!" Invariably, those who do discover that this approach really does work, because they are immutable laws based on our God-given human nature.

So, when you are sharing the Gospel with others, be aware of the Four Stages as you apply the Eight Laws. If you apply these principles consistently, I guarantee that you will become an effective evangelist in all areas of your life.

6

JESUS: THE PERFECT EVANGELIST

During His earthly ministry, Jesus devoted Himself to a small group of men, known as the apostles. To prepare them to follow Him, Jesus did the following:

- Called them to His mission (Jn 15:16; Mk 13:13–39; Lk 6:13–16);

- Individually discipled them (Acts 1:21–22);

- Gave them the gift of the Holy Spirit and the divine authority to carry on His ministry and His mission (Mt 2:18–20; 10:8–14; Mk 3:13–16; 6:7–13; 16:15; Lk 9:2ff; 24:47; etc.).

Today Jesus is counting on you to run the race and, like His first disciples, to carry the baton of His Good News to the next generation. If you don't, who will? Our Lord founded the Catholic Church, and called you to be part of it, to ensure that His work would continue throughout the ages.

Jesus established the Church to teach, govern, and sanctify the people of God. The members of this divinely established community have handed on the Catholic and apostolic Faith throughout the subsequent centuries to people all over the world. Let me underline this important truth: Jesus' primary evangelization objective in His earthly ministry was to found and to form His Catholic Church in order to be present with us in the Mass and the other sacraments until He comes again in glory. Thank you, Jesus!

Jesus and the Eight Laws

Obviously the greatest evangelist of all was our Lord Himself. Did Jesus employ the Eight Laws outlined in the last chapter? The answer is an unqualified yes! Let's take a look at how our Lord applied these timeless principles:

1. Keep It Simple

It is good to remember that the Gospel was delivered to the simple: shepherds, fishermen, widows, the sick, the poor, and so forth. Jesus often taught in parables, which is a fancy way of saying that He told stories. Most often His stories were about everyday people and activities: a farmer sowing seed, a poor woman who lost a coin, day laborers working in a vineyard, guests at a wedding party, a lost sheep, and so on. To convey profound divine truths Jesus told simple stories to which simple people could relate.

2. Keep Him Saying Yes

As I said before, establishing common ground is very important when sharing the Faith. An effective way to do this is by asking questions or making statements with which others will agree. Jesus used this principle often. One striking example occurs in the Sermon on the Mount (Mt 5–7). In His teaching on anger, adultery, divorce, taking oaths, retaliation, love of enemies, and almsgiving (Mt 5:17–48)

Jesus begins each topic with the words "You have heard that it was said . . ." and an Old Testament teaching that He knows His listeners all accept. Then He goes on, "But I say to you . . ." and proceeds to evangelize the crowd about the deeper responsibilities of obedience to God. This is a powerful example of Jesus' use of the principle "Keep him saying yes."

3. Be Enthusiastic

We can see the enthusiasm of Jesus throughout His teaching and preaching. He is without doubt the most dynamic individual who ever lived. When Jesus drove the buyers and sellers from the Temple, "his disciples recalled the words of Scripture, 'Zeal for your house will consume me'" (Jn 2:17).

Enthusiasm doesn't mean constant shouting or endless activity, however, but rather letting your passion show through your words and actions. Recall that *enthusiasm* means "God is in you." Clearly there can be no greater example of this than our Lord Jesus, who is called Emmanuel, which means "God is with us" (cf. Mt 1:23; Isa 7:14).

4. Call Him by Name

Names were very important in the ancient world, just as they are today. Not surprisingly, Jesus called people by name, but none more so than Simon Peter. At their first meeting Jesus says, "You are Simon the son of John; you will be called Cephas (which is translated Peter)" (Jn 1:42). In the Gospels, our Lord calls Simon Peter by name more than He does any other person (e.g., Mt 16:17–18, 17:25; Lk 22:31; Jn 21:15–17).

In the Old Testament, God changed Abram's name to Abraham when He commissioned the great patriarch to be our father in faith. Likewise, in the New Testament, Jesus changed Simon's name to Peter when He made him the earthly head of the Church. Clearly Jesus considered calling people by name very significant.

5. Show and Then Tell

Jesus used the principle "Show and then tell" when the Jewish leaders asked if it was lawful to pay taxes to Caesar (Mk 12:14–17). Jesus said, "Bring me a denarius to look at." When they produced the coin He asked, "Whose image and inscription is this?" That was the "show". They replied, "Caesar's." Then He explained, "Repay to Caesar what belongs to Caesar and to God what belongs to God." That was the "tell".

Another time His disciples asked, "Who is the greatest in the kingdom of heaven?" To illustrate how much He values humility, Jesus put a child in their midst (the "show") and said, "Whoever humbles himself like this child is the greatest in the kingdom of heaven" (the "tell") (Mt 18:1, 4).

The principle "Show and then tell" is also apparent in the way Jesus would perform a miracle and then explain its significance. For example, the miracle of the loaves and fishes (the "show") was followed by the Bread of Life discourse (the "tell") in John 6:1–15, 22–59.

6. Always Agree

In the Bible Jesus says, "Agree quickly with your adversary" (Mt 5:25 KJV). As I said before, this does not mean watering down your message but rather letting your listeners know that you understand what they are saying. For example, when a scholar of the law answers our Lord correctly that love of God and neighbor is the greatest commandment, Jesus agrees: "You have answered correctly; do this and you will live" (cf. Lk 10:25–28). This is simple agreement.

Now consider the words of Jesus to the Samaritan woman at the well. When the woman tells Him, "I have no husband", Jesus agrees: "You are right in saying, 'I do not have a husband.'" But then He continues, "For you have had five husbands and the one you have now is not your husband. What you have said is true." Again, Jesus agrees but obviously does not approve. Rather He demonstrates powerfully that He truly understands (cf. Jn 4:17–18).

7. Ask Questions

It is already abundantly clear from the previous examples that Jesus loved to ask questions. Powerful questions accompany one personal encounter with the Lord after another: "Can the wedding guests mourn as long as the bridegroom is with them?" (Mt 9:15); "Who is my mother? Who are my brothers?" (Mt 12:48b); "Can any of you by worrying add a single moment to your life-span?" (Mt 6:27); "Which one of you would hand his son a stone when he asks for a loaf of bread, or a snake when he asks for a fish?" (Mt 7:9–10); "But who do you say that I am?" (Mt 16:15). These are only a few examples taken from one of the four Gospels. There are countless other important questions that Jesus asked in order to help people understand His mission. When they honestly answered His questions—even if only in their hearts—they were obliged to admit the truth of His message.

8. Practice Virtue

Of course Jesus is the perfect model of this law of evange-lization. The Scripture tells us that Jesus became like us in all things except sin (cf. Phil 2:7; Heb 2:17), and our Lord's perfect example of personal virtue was so well established that He could openly challenge His enemies with the ques-tion "Can any of you charge me with sin?" (Jn 8:46).

Even when His human nature recoiled at the prospect of His Passion, Jesus prayed to the Father, "Not my will, but yours be done" (Lk 22:42b). Jesus always practiced virtue and lived in the presence of God, and He calls us to do the same. "So be perfect, just as your heavenly Father is perfect" (Mt 5:48).

Clearly our Lord Jesus Christ most effectively utilized all of these immutable Eight Laws when sharing His Good News—and you should too.

7

PLANTING SEEDS FOR JESUS

Jesus told this parable about spreading the Good News about God:

> The sower sows God's message. Some people are like the seeds that fall along the path; as soon as they hear the message, Satan comes and takes it away. Other people are like the seeds that fall on rocky ground. As soon as they hear the message, they receive it gladly. But it does not sink deep into them, and they don't last long. So when trouble or persecution comes because of the message, they give up at once. Other people are like the seeds sown among the thorn bushes. These are the ones who hear the message, but the worries about this life, the love for riches, and all other kinds of desires crowd in and choke the message, and they don't bear fruit. But other people are like seeds sown in good soil. They hear the message, accept it, and bear fruit: some thirty, some sixty, and some one hundred. (Mk 4:14–20, GNT)

I mentioned before that often the most we can hope for in evangelization is to plant a seed. So many times the window of opportunity for evangelization is so short that your witness is just a smile, a kind word, or a helping hand. This is the fruit of living in the presence of God and is a living witness to the motto of Saint Francis of Assisi: "Preach the Gospel always; if necessary, use words." Other times God provides us with the opportunity to share more when sowing his message. Let me give you three examples of planting seeds from my own life.

"Officer Mike"

This first example took place at the Sacred Heart Chapel in Covina, California. The Catholic Resource Center (of which I am president) moved into this century-old chapel in 2003. Over the years, many people have seen the outer restoration and have been curious to see the interior. One day I saw two policemen standing outside, admiring the building. They told me that they remembered coming to this church during their childhood, so I offered to give them a tour.

As I showed them around, I got the impression that one of them, "Officer Mike", was no longer a practicing Catholic. So after the tour I gave them both some CDs on the Catholic Faith and invited them to come back for Sunday Mass. I also invited them to attend a mission we were having that week with a Franciscan priest. I was just planting a seed.

Later I took my kids to a fast-food place and Officer Mike just happened to be there. He said, "Hey, do you have a few minutes?"

So we sat down, and over lunch he asked me a very profound question: "What happens when you die?" He continued, "How are you judged? What takes place?" I gave him a brief explanation of the particular and general judgments like one you would find in a basic catechism. Then he said to me, "You might think that cops live good moral lives, but let me tell you, I've messed up my life big time! My marriage has fallen apart, and I'm really hurting."

Knowing he was a non-practicing Catholic I said, "Come to the mission at the chapel today, and go to confession. Start over with a clean slate."

He said, "I'm afraid that if I go to confession, the priest is going to kick my butt!"

I leaned over the table and looked him right in the eye: "Mike, maybe you need your butt kicked."

He sighed, "Maybe I do", and left.

I was afraid that Mike might just chicken out, so I immediately called an elderly couple I know who are strong in their Catholic faith. The wife is dying of cancer, and the husband is sick too. I asked them to pray for this man so that he could receive the grace of confession and return to the practice of the Faith. They offered their prayers and sufferings for him that afternoon.

After Mike left the restaurant, he went straight to the chapel to go to confession. The line was very long. Seeing Mike's uniform, one of our guys offered to move him forward in the line. "I don't want to cut off anyone already waiting in line", he said. "I'll come back after my shift at 6:30."

He did return that evening, but the line was still very long. He waited in my office, getting more and more nervous. Three times he nearly left. Finally he said, "I'll just try another time. You know, it has been twenty-five years since my last confession; I don't even remember what to do. What would I say?"

I told him, "Just tell the priest how long it has been and describe to him what you have gone through in the past twenty-five years of your life."

I saw Mike enter the confessional and had to leave immediately for the airport to make my flight for a weekend conference.

After the conference, I took a red-eye flight home and arrived on Sunday at one in the morning. I told Danielle, "I'm going to the first Mass this morning to offer the Holy Sacrifice in thanksgiving for Mike's return to the state of grace." At that 6:30 Mass, when I looked up from my prayers, who was kneeling next to me in the pew? Officer Mike had come home. He received Holy Communion that morning for the first time in twenty-five years.

After Mass he said to me, "I felt like I was walking on air when I received Communion. I am at peace with my God."

This was a case where planting a seed quickly and powerfully bore fruit, but like a real farmer, you will usually not see such immediate results of your seed planting.

Senior Discount

Here is another example. I was in line at a fast-food restaurant, and the lady ahead of me asked for the senior discount. When it was my turn to order, I asked how old you had to be to get the senior discount. The young woman behind the counter told me, "Fifty years old."

I said, "Well, I guess I qualify, because I'm fifty-five. Boy, am I glad to be a senior!"

She looked at me in shock and said, "Being older is nothing to be happy about! You're closer to the end."

I read her name tag and asked a question. "Rosa, can I break some news to you? No one gets out alive! I'm happy because I know who I am in Christ and *where I'm going* at the end. Life is short, but eternity is forever."

Then I moved along to let the next customer order. That was it. I have no idea what impact this little exchange may have had on that young woman. As happens so often in evangelization, I could only plant the seed and hope for the best.

Cell Phone

Another time, a friend asked me to help him clean out a commercial building he owned that was about to be foreclosed. He rented a forty-foot dumpster, which we proceeded to fill with trash. The new owner of the building, who wanted us out quick—and frankly was not being very nice about it—was standing by when he accidentally dropped his cell phone into that forty-foot dumpster! Well, he proceeded to swear a blue streak and to blaspheme the name of our Lord.

I felt sorry for the man and asked my guardian angel, "What can I do to help him?"

What did I do? I told the man, "Don't worry. We know it's in here. I'll get your phone for you. We'll just keep calling your phone to hear the ring, and I'll find it."

I rummaged through the trash for about fifteen minutes before I finally found the cell phone and held it up. "Here it is!"

The man's look of relief signaled to me an opportunity to plant a seed, so I asked him a question: "Why don't we take a moment to say a prayer of thanks to God for finding your phone?"

His reaction could not have surprised me more. The expression on his face changed instantly from relief to bewildered revulsion at my suggestion. Then he stormed off saying words I won't repeat. I was sorry for him, not because he didn't thank me, but because he rejected an opportunity to thank God.

In each of these examples we see how "man proposes, but God disposes." It is our duty to share the Good News as best we can, but while we may plant the seed, what happens in people's hearts is beyond our control. The simple fact is that no matter how much or how well we evangelize, human beings have the free will to choose whether they will cooperate with the grace of God. As Venerable Fulton Sheen used to say, "The only value in saying yes to God is that you have the freedom to say no."

As evangelists we must also remember that our reaching out may be only one thread in the rich tapestry being woven by the will of God in someone else's life. In the end it is He who does the converting.

8

THE TEN COMMANDMENTS
OF EVANGELIZATION

Our duty to bear witness to the death and resurrection of
Jesus and His saving presence in our lives is as real and
pressing as was the duty of the first disciples.

—Pope Blessed John Paul II, "Message for
World Communications Day", June 4, 2000

This chapter introduces ten rules for effective evangelization
that I have practiced successfully for many years. As with the
Eight Laws of Sharing the Faith with Anyone, the following
Ten Commandments of Evangelization are tried-and-true,
proven-effective rules to make your efforts at sharing the
Faith more fruitful:

1. Thou shalt pray always.
2. Thou shalt be prepared.
3. Thou shalt be intentional.
4. Thou shalt not get discouraged.
5. Thou shalt stay motivated.
6. Thou shalt be kind.
7. Thou shalt ask questions.
8. Thou shalt admit when thou art wrong.
9. Thou shalt reap what thou sow.
10. Be not afraid.

Along with an explanation of each of these are a number of evangelization stories that illustrate how they work in the real world.

1. Thou Shalt Pray Always

As I explain in detail in another chapter, a life of prayer —including regular prayer before the Blessed Sacrament— must be your first priority as an evangelist. You should always begin and end each faith-sharing encounter with prayer. Be sure to pray to your guardian angel to help set the stage for your evangelization. Whenever possible you should also pray with the person or persons with whom you are sharing the Faith. This is especially effective when you deal with Bible-believing Christians. The fact that they have met a Catholic who prays and knows his Faith will go a long way in altering their opinion of Catholics and the Church.

I heartily recommend that you read *The Soul of the Apostolate* by Jean-Baptiste Chautard, which powerfully presents the need to develop profound spirituality before you go out to evangelize. Of course, I also recommend reading the Bible daily, but I ask you to remember the admonition of Saint Francis Assisi to pray more than you read.

2. Thou Shalt Be Prepared

"Always be ready to give an explanation to anyone who asks you for a reason for your hope, but do it with gentleness and reverence" (1 Pet 3:15b–16a). Being prepared to share your Faith requires study. You do not have to be an expert, but you should know the basics, and that means spending time with the Bible and the *Catechism*. It is also crucial to study apologetics—the science of defending the Faith.

Saint Joseph Communications has many CDs on apologetics as well as a book called *Basic Apologetics* that answers many common objections to Catholicism, but, for an evangelist, apologetics is really the study of a lifetime. I recommend that you start by getting a good study Bible. Of course, you should get a Catholic Bible and be sure it is one you do not mind writing in (that is to say, not a family heirloom). As you read books, visit websites, and listen to apologetics CDs, be sure to highlight key verses in your Bible and make pertinent notes in the margins.

You should also memorize key verses. Knowing important parts of the Bible by heart ensures that you will always have your most important biblical evidence with you, even if you do not have your Bible. Do not be intimidated by the prospect of memorization. You already know many prayers, such as the Apostles' Creed, that are longer than almost any Bible verse you will care to memorize. Other prayers you have already committed to memory, or parts of them, actually come straight from the Bible: the Hail Mary (Lk 1:28, 42), the Our Father (Mt 6:9–13), and the Magnificat (Lk 1:46–55), for instance.

A young fellow from Wichita, Kansas, called to thank me for the Midwest Family Conference. He said, "I have been studying the Bible and apologetics. This summer I went to a nondenominational Bible summer camp." The first day, he introduced himself to the group by identifying his church as Saint Mary's.

"You're Catholic?" they asked. "Catholics worship Mary!"

He smiled and said, "That's not really what the Catholic Church teaches" and proceeded to evangelize his separated brothers and sisters.

What makes this story unique is not just that a Catholic would enter a nondenominational "lions' den" to share his Faith, but that this young fellow was only ten years old! If he can do it, so can you.

3. Thou Shalt Be Intentional

I often say that evangelism is an attitude. Jesus told Peter and other apostles that He would make them "fishers of men" (Mt 4:19), and He compared Himself to a farmer sowing seeds (Mt 13:1–9). God will put you in situations that will give you the opportunity to evangelize. The point of being intentional is to seize those opportunities, because fish do not catch themselves and someone has to plant the seeds!

Another example of seed planting from my life was the time my son Joseph and I visited the Grand Canyon for a Catholic father-son campout. The weekend started with a thirty-mile hike. At one point, we climbed down the side of the canyon with a rope to get a spectacular view of Havasu Falls. We were joined by a group of eight pierced, tattooed, rough-looking fellows who were using even rougher language. Now, there we were, a group of Catholic men with our sons, so I asked my guardian angel, "How do we evangelize a bunch like this who is using bad language in front of the boys?"

Then I smiled and said, "Hey, can I ask you fellas a question? Can you tell me who built this waterfall? Was it a construction company from Phoenix or LA?" Of course they did not answer; they just looked at me as if I were crazy, so I let them off the hook: "Wouldn't you guys agree that God made this waterfall and, for that matter, the whole canyon?" They agreed, so I went on: "Do you guys think it's a good idea to thank God for this beautiful view we're experiencing?" Once again, they agreed. So I told them, "Good. You guys have a great day."

It may not have been much, but in this way I was able to give them at least some message. What is more, they cleaned up their language, and I did not have to tell them to clean it up. I just brought God into the picture, and they got the message.

Something similar happened when I took the kids to a game at Angel Stadium. It was a "rivalry game", and some of the fans were pretty worked up. Coming back to our seats with hot dogs and Cokes for the kids, I saw a fight breaking out between two men, one of whom had obviously had too much to drink. How do you evangelize someone like that?

Well, I stepped in and told him he should cool down, but at five-foot-five and 135 pounds, I am not very intimidating.

So he asked, "Oh yeah? What are you going to do about it?"

I looked at him with a smile and answered, "I'm going to say a prayer that you stop drinking and that you get home to your wife and family safely."

He looked at me and said, "Thank you. You're right. I shouldn't be doing this."

He took his seat, did not use any more bad language—or have any more to drink—and was a model fan for the rest of the game. I did not need to hit him over the head with the Gospel; I did not need to get physical; I just smiled and offered to pray for him.

In both these cases, I could have remained silent, but because I have the intention to share Christ, by word and example, God was able to use me at least to plant a seed.

4. Thou Shalt Not Get Discouraged

Sharing the Faith is not a "numbers game". We read in the Bible about Peter's first sermon, on Pentecost: "Those who accepted his message were baptized, and about three thousand persons were added that day" (Acts 2:14–41). Five chapters later we read the discourse of Saint Stephen (Acts 7), who gave his testimony before the high priest and the Sanhedrin, but with quite a different result. We read in verse 54, "When they heard this they were infuriated, and ground their teeth at him." Stephen was stoned to death and became the first Christian martyr.

Peter and Stephen were both filled with the Spirit and faithful to the call, but with very different results. As Blessed Mother Teresa of Calcutta said, "God doesn't require you to succeed; He only requires that you try."

In the 1980s disgraced televangelist Jimmy Swaggart led an anti-Catholic crusade on his weekly Pentecostal television show in order to get Catholics "saved". In 1985 he wrote the 54-page booklet *An Open Letter to My Catholic Friends*, a blatant attack on Catholic doctrines that accused the Church of being "anti-Bible and anti-God". His followers would put it on cars outside Catholic churches and in other places in an effort to persuade the faithful to leave the Church. Many Catholics did leave the Church. Frankly, it was discouraging.

In response, Catholic evangelist Father Ken Roberts wrote a little book called *Father Roberts Answers Jimmy Swaggart*. I was still in real estate at the time, so I had seventy-five thousand copies of his book printed—in English and in Spanish —and gave them away free.

At this time a local Calvary Chapel announced that a fallen-away priest would be giving an anti-Catholic presentation there. They invited Catholics to come and to "learn the truth" about "the errors" of Catholicism. So I got my buddies together, and we sat outside Calvary Chapel handing out Father Roberts' book and saying, "Tonight's topic is Catholicism; here's your free book." Naturally they took us for members of Calvary Chapel! We gave out about twelve hundred books.

The chapel was packed, and the fallen-away priest told many falsehoods about the Church. It was pretty brutal. I held up my hand during the Q&A, but the fallen-away priest wouldn't call on me. Finally he called on another guy and asked him, "Do you have a question?"

"No," he replied, "but my good friend Terry Barber has one!"

So I got up and said, "You've pointed out a bunch of so-called errors of Catholicism, but a kid in third-grade catechism class knows that what you're claiming is not the teaching of the Church." I went on to point out several specific examples. Then I asked the audience, "Would any of you go to a deserter to find out about the army? Then don't go to this man to learn about Catholicism! Go to Bishop Fulton Sheen! I have thousands of his tapes in the parking lot, and I'll be happy to give them to you for free."

Well, the next thing I knew, the lights started flickering and four guys came up and grabbed me—one on each arm and one on each leg—carried me out of the church, and threw me out into the parking lot. Now, I might have gotten discouraged at this point and left, but I stayed, just in case anyone might want to talk to me. Suddenly, all the people started coming out of the church. I had shut the whole talk down! I was in that parking lot giving out tapes and answering questions about the Catholic Faith until one in the morning! It pays not to get discouraged.

5. Thou Shalt Stay Motivated

"Therefore, since we are surrounded by so great a cloud of witnesses, let us rid ourselves of every burden and sin that clings to us and persevere in running the race that lies before us while keeping our eyes fixed on Jesus, the leader and perfecter of faith" (Heb 12:1–2a).

To stay motivated you should always remember you are not alone. Reading the lives of saints, listening to Catholic CDs and Catholic radio, and watching EWTN and Catholic DVDs are all ways to stay motivated through the encouraging example of powerful evangelists. It is also important to remember the stakes. As Jesus says, "For what shall it profit a man, if he shall gain the whole world, and lose his own soul?" (Mark 8:36, KJV). Jesus shows us just how much souls are worth to God with the parables of the lost sheep, the lost coin, and the prodigal son, which are found in the Gospel of Luke. Meditating on how important souls are to Jesus will help you stay motivated.

I often ask people—and myself: What will you do today that will matter one hundred years from now? You and I will be dead. The kind of house you lived in or the kind of car you drove will not matter at all. But the souls you touched in this life and helped to bring back to God will matter a lot.

Do you have any friends or relatives who have left the Catholic Church? I do. Can you guess what has been the most effective method of spiritual motivation in the two-thousand-year history of the Catholic Church? It is meditation on the four last things: death, judgment, heaven, and hell. Scripture tells us that God "wills everyone to be saved and to come to knowledge of the truth" (1 Tim 2:4). I hope and pray that all my friends and relatives—especially my four kids—get to heaven; just the fact that they might not motivates me to try all the harder.

6. Thou Shalt Be Kind

"If you are earnestly conforming yourself to the image of Jesus Christ, sharpness, bitterness, and sarcasm disappear. The very attempt to be like Jesus is already a source of sweetness within you, flowing with an easy grace over all who come within your reach."

I've said it before, and I'll say it again: "People don't care how much you know until they know how much you care." Be kind. Don't be a bully or come off like a know-it-all. Evangelization is about saving souls—bringing souls to

Christ and bringing our separated brethren into the fullness of the Faith. I have seen great evangelists like Tim Staples and Scott Hahn stay for hours after a talk to answer people's questions. I think those people know how much these evangelists care for them.

Of course, no one cares more for souls than our Lord Himself. Did you know that according to the four Gospels, Jesus performed 75 percent of His miracles for people who interrupted Him? Obviously Jesus thinks souls are worth our time. Remember my story about the little boy who tugged on my pants leg to ask, "Do you know who made you?" He was interrupting me. But I would not trade that experience for anything. That little fellow evangelized me! But it never would have happened if I had not allowed him to interrupt me.

Also remember always to smile, whether you feel like it or not. A smile costs you nothing but can do so much good. Take the advice of Father Lovasik: "Become a member of the *Apostolate of Smiling*. Your smile has work to do for God, because it is an instrument for winning souls. Sanctifying grace, dwelling in your soul, will sweeten your smile and will enable it to do much good."

7. Thou Shalt Ask Questions

I have told you this already, but it bears repeating: "He who asks questions has control." Here are two more examples of the importance of asking questions.

I was once approached by a pair of Mormon missionaries. I noticed they were both Hispanic, so I asked, "By any chance, were you guys once Catholics?"

"Yes", they replied.

"Oh, really?" I said. "How well did you know your Catholic Faith?"

"Oh, we knew all about it", was their confident response. "We were altar boys and went to Catholic school."

"Well then," I went on innocently, "do you mind if I ask you guys a couple of questions?"

"No, go ahead."

"Can you name the seven sacraments?" They could not. "How about the Ten Commandments?" Again, no answer. I said, "I don't understand. I thought you knew all about Catholicism."

Then I called over my (at the time) seven-year-old son. "Johnny, can you name the seven sacraments?" He did. "What about the Ten Commandments?" Again, no problem. The Mormons started to look worried, and I said, "Gentlemen, you don't seem to know as much about Catholicism as my seven-year-old. Could it be that you have rejected not the Catholic Faith but your own poor understanding of the Catholic Faith? I suggest you investigate what you have given up before you start preaching against it."

They said quickly, "Well, we can't talk anymore; we have an appointment."

I knew my time was up, so I said in parting, "Let me ask you one more question. Mormons claim the Church went apostate in the early centuries. Did you know that Christ promised Peter that 'the gates of hell will not prevail against' His Church [Mt 16:18] and that He further promised, 'I will be with you all days even to the end of the world' [Mt

28:20b]? If the Church went apostate, then Christ broke His promise, and I think you'll agree He would not do that."

I did not have to come down hard on those Mormon missionaries. I just asked them questions to demonstrate that they had left something they did not really know.

This is the approach I also take with those who say, "I don't need you to tell me about Catholicism; I survived twelve years of Catholic school." When they cannot name the sacraments or the commandments I suggest, "Since you rejected the Church as a kid, maybe it wasn't really the Church you rejected but your childish idea of the Church."

On another occasion I was visiting one of my vendors, and I noticed there were impure images on some of the computer screen savers. I asked a young woman in the office, "Doesn't that offend your dignity as a woman?" She agreed that it did, so I asked, "Have you told the boss how you feel?" She said that she had but that he didn't think it was a big deal.

When the boss came out of the back I called him by name and asked, "Nick, don't you agree those screen savers are pornographic and an insult to the dignity of women? Would you like it if that was a picture of your daughter?"

"No," he admitted, "I wouldn't."

"Well then, Nick, you run this place. Get rid of those images! Be a real man. Men are supposed to protect women and defend their dignity. Don't be a wimp. Get rid of them!" Please understand that I have known this man for twenty years, and I am comfortable speaking to him in this way.

He thought about it and said, "I guess you're right", and he got rid of the impure images on the computers.

When I go into that office today, the women still thank me. I tell them what Bishop Sheen used to say: "Any good we do comes from God, and we thank Him for it." This is just another example of the good that can come from asking questions.

8. Thou Shalt Admit When Thou Art Wrong

Many Catholics are concerned about not being able to answer questions; if you are, you must not let that keep you from evangelizing. The solution to this is simple. If you don't know the answer to a question, just admit it, promise to get back to the person who asked the question, and then go find the answer. This requires humility, but it is the right thing to do. I can guarantee that even well-known apologists like Tim Staples and Pat Madrid have been stumped plenty of times; I most certainly have. It is not a weakness; it is an opportunity to grow. So don't feel as if you need to have all the answers. You do not have to be perfect, just humble. People will pick up on your honesty. They will realize that you are not out just to win an argument but that you really care about being a witness for your Faith.

I remember hearing from a young college girl who had never been formally catechized. Some Evangelical Protestant friends at school attacked her Catholic Faith. Not knowing how to answer, she wound up in tears. But the following Sunday she found Tim Staples' CD *Teen Apologetics* in the Lighthouse Catholic Media kiosk in the back of her parish church. It had all the answers she was looking for! She went back to school on Monday empowered with solid, biblical responses to all of her friends' objections.

Instead of losing her faith, like millions of other college kids, she started studying the *Catechism* and learning apologetics and got involved in a Catholic campus ministry to help others like her to know and defend their Faith. And it is all because she took the time to go find out.

9. Thou Shalt Reap What Thou Sow

I have shared my opinion that personal contact is important in evangelization, but it is not always possible. So I am also a big promoter of handing out literature and CDs on the Catholic Faith, which I carry with me. Saint Alphonsus Liguori said, "Only God knows how much good can come from a holy book." I apply that to CDs and DVDs as well. I have read that 53 percent of those who have come back to the Church were given some kind of written or recorded materials. I am not surprised. As Scott Hahn says, "The Catholic Church is like a caged lion. It does not need defending; it just needs to be let out." Sometimes a book or a CD is the key to unlock the cage.

If you are familiar with Dr. Hahn's journey into the Church, you know how a proper understanding of contraception played an important role in the conversion of his wife, Kimberly. Once at a fundraising picnic a lady came up to me and asked, "Are you Terry Barber?" Now, when people ask me that question I never know whether I am in for a pat on the back or a slap in the face, but I pleaded guilty, and she went on: "Eleven years ago I was away from the Church, and my father sent me Scott Hahn's conversion tape. My husband and I were not practicing our Faith, and we were contracepting. That tape brought us back to the Church. Now I'd like to introduce you to my five kids." Wow. And it was all because her dad sent her a tape.

Another powerful example: a man came up to me at a conference and said, "I want to thank you for saving my life." I did not know this young man from Adam, so I asked what he was talking about. He said he had been addicted to drugs and alcohol, lost his job and his wife, and was going to commit suicide. He put the barrel of a loaded .357 Magnum in his mouth and was ready to pull the trigger. What stopped him? His mom had sent him a CD we produced on the lordship of Christ, by Jesse Romero.

The young man told me, "I decided, before I kill myself, I'll put on that CD so when they find me they'll know I was listening to it, and that will console my mom." So he listened to the first CD and then another and then the rest. And as he listened, he got fired up about life and inspired to know Jesus Christ. He said, "For a full year I studied the Bible and the *Catechism* and ordered more and more CDs from Saint Joseph's." Then he dropped the bombshell: "Today I am a seminarian in formation to be a Catholic priest!"

Thanks be to God and to this young man's mom for sending him those CDs.

10. Be Not Afraid

To overcome fear of evangelization we all need three things: devotion to our Lord, especially in the Blessed Sacrament; devotion to His Most Blessed Mother; and unfailing loyalty to His Vicar on earth, our Holy Father, the Pope. Jesus says, "Go and make disciples" (Mt 28:19); Mary says, "Do whatever he tells you" (Jn 2:5); Pope Francis says, "The Spirit of the Risen Christ drove out fear from the apostles' hearts and impelled them to leave the Upper Room in order to spread the Gospel. Let us too have greater courage in witnessing to our faith in the Risen Christ! We must not be afraid of being Christian and living as Christians! We must have this courage to go and proclaim the Risen Christ."

Pope Benedict XVI also exhorted us to evangelize, and one of the key themes of John Paul II's long pontificate was the New Evangelization. The motto he chose for this project was "Be not afraid."

I have a special love for JP II and consider him worthy of the title John Paul the Great. I started Saint Joseph Communications in 1979, the year he was elected Pope. I try always to follow his biblical prescription "Be not afraid." Did you know that the phrase "Be not afraid" appears in the Bible 365 times? That's once for each day of the year. "For God did not give us a spirit of cowardice but rather of power and love and self-control" (2 Tim 1:7).

By the grace of God I have helped bring many people into—or back into—the Catholic Church. People ask me, "How do you do it?" The answer is this: I keep trying. I fail a lot. I fail nine times out of ten, but I just keep trying. And if the thing I am trying does not work, I try something else. Anyone can go into a corner and say, "I don't care. I'm just going to say my prayers and forget everybody else." But choosing not to act has its consequences. As Bishop Sheen said, "Even dead bodies float downstream." I for one am not content to go with the flow. You do not need to have all the answers. You do not need to see instant results. If you are out there sowing the seeds, God will use others to water them. You need only to stay faithful and to be not afraid.

9

THE HEART OF EVANGELIZATION

No book on sharing the Catholic Faith would be complete without acknowledging the importance of the Blessed Virgin Mary: Mother of Jesus, model Christian, and Mother of the Church. Catholics believe that the meaning and purpose of life is to know, to love, and to serve God in this world and to be happy with Him forever in heaven. No one on this earth ever knew Jesus better, or loved Him more, than His Blessed Mother. At the end of her earthly life, Mary took her place beside her Divine Son as Queen of Heaven. But how did Mary see herself? In the first chapter of Luke's Gospel, Mary twice refers to herself as the "servant" of the Lord (Lk 1:38, 48).

The Qualities of a Servant

Let's look at the qualities of a servant as we see them in Mary:

Prepared by God

We can discern the qualities of servanthood especially in Mary's encounter with the angel Gabriel (Lk 1:26–38) and in her canticle of praise, the Magnificat (Lk 1:46–55). In Luke 1:28, the angel says to Mary, "Hail, favored one! The

Lord is with you." Mary was preserved from original sin and filled with the grace of God in a special way so that she might be prepared for her special mission in life. We, in turn, are freed from original sin and filled with God's grace at baptism and confirmation for the same reason: that we may be prepared for our mission of sharing the Gospel.

Called for a Specific Mission

God called Mary for a specific mission: to bring Jesus, the Word, into the world. Christians are called to do likewise; we "give birth" to Christ in people's lives through evangelization. The Catholic Church links the mission of the faithful to that of Mary: Mary gave us Jesus; Jesus gave us the Mass; the Mass gives us the Eucharist through the hands of the priest; we who benefit from all these gifts are called to share them with others. The Lord has chosen us to be ambassadors for His Bride, the Church. Like Mary, we have been chosen by Him for a specific mission.

Filled with the Spirit

The Holy Spirit is present with the Lord's servant. When Mary asked the angel how it could be that she, a virgin, would give birth to the Savior, the angel said, "The Holy Spirit will come upon you, and the power of the Most High will overshadow you" (Lk 1:35). Our mission of evangelization is also accomplished by the Holy Spirit. Like Mary, we participate in this great work because God has chosen "earthen vessels" to show that the transcendent power belongs to Him and not to us (cf. 2 Cor 4:7). Abandoning ourselves to the power of the Holy Spirit as Mary did (Lk 1:38) gives us the grace to serve out of charity, or love of God.

Confident in God

The angel Gabriel told Mary that her cousin Elizabeth was also going to have a baby. Elizabeth was old and childless, but the angel told Mary, "Nothing will be impossible for God" (Lk 1:37). Not only did Elizabeth give birth, but her baby grew up to be Saint John the Baptist, the forerunner of Jesus who would "prepare the way of the Lord" with his preaching (Mk 1:3). As the angel had told Mary, Jesus Himself told the apostles, "For God, all things are possible" (Mt 19:26). These verses remind us that to evangelize well we must remember that the task ahead of us is never as great as the power behind us.

Obedient to the Lord

Mary showed her obedience to God when she answered the angel, "Behold, I am the handmaid of the Lord. May it be done to me according to your word" (Lk 1:38). Our Lady was entirely obedient because her faith was rooted in God's promises; as we read in her Magnificat: "He has helped Israel his servant, remembering his mercy, according to his promise to our fathers, to Abraham and to his descendants forever" (Lk 1:54-55). Mary, the Mother of Jesus, was the first disciple and evangelist. She calls us to obedience through her words to the servants at the wedding at Cana, "Do whatever he tells you" (Jn 2:5).

No Mary, No Jesus—Know Mary, Know Jesus

"To know Jesus Christ and his love causes us to want to share that knowledge and love with everyone we meet" (Archbishop José Horacio Gomez, *You Will Be My Witnesses*).

If Mary had not said yes to the angel Gabriel, there would have been no Incarnation of Jesus. Thanks be to God, she cooperated with His grace, but it was truly her free choice. That is why we can say, "No Mary, no Jesus." Through her Yes to God, Mary became the human being closest to the Blessed Trinity: the Beloved Daughter of God the Father; the Most Chaste Spouse of God the Holy Spirit; and the Blessed Mother of God the Son. Catholic Christians know that one of the best ways to stay close to Jesus is through the powerful intercession of the one who knew Him best. And so we say not only, "No Mary, no Jesus", but also, "Know Mary, know Jesus." If we imitate Mary in her obedience, her love, and especially her willingness to serve and to share Jesus with the world, we can hope to join her and her Divine Son in heaven. In this way Mary continues to evangelize us. We in turn, evangelize others. As Scott Hahn once said, "Evangelism is not complete until the evangelized become evangelists."

Light from the Word

Keep your focus on the Lord

"And Mary said: 'My soul proclaims the greatness of the Lord; my spirit rejoices in God my savior'" (Lk 1:46–47).

"But seek first the kingdom (of God) and his righteousness, and all these things will be given you besides" (Mt 6:33).

"Therefore, we aspire to please him" (2 Cor 5:9a).

Abandon yourself to the Holy Spirit

"The holy Spirit will come upon you, and the power of the Most High will overshadow you" (Lk 1:35).

"But you will receive power when the holy Spirit comes upon you, and you will be my witnesses in Jerusalem, throughout Judea and Samaria, and to the ends of the earth" (Acts 1:8).

Fall in love with God and practice obedience

"Behold, I am the handmaid of the Lord. May it be done to me according to your word" (Lk 1:38).

"Whoever is without love does not know God, for God is love. . . . In this is love: not that we have loved God, but that he loved us" (1 Jn 4:8, 10).

"Since you have purified yourselves by obedience to the truth for sincere mutual love, love one another intensely from a [pure] heart" (1 Pet 1:22).

HOW TO SHARE YOUR
PERSONAL TESTIMONY

Modern man listens more willingly to witnesses
than to teachers, and if he does listen to teachers,
it is because they are witnesses.

—Pope Venerable Paul VI, *On
Evangelization in the Modern World*

You may have noticed that I like to tell stories. Our Lord
Himself often communicated the Good News by telling stories, and it is good for us to follow His example. There are
many sources for the stories we may use: Scripture, the lives
of the saints, popular Catholic books and CDs, and so forth.
But personal stories are the best. And the most compelling
story you can tell is your own.

Saint Paul used personal faith stories and spoke to others about his life and conversion. It was a dynamic way to
evangelize and a natural—and extremely effective—way for
him to communicate God's intervention in his life (cf. Acts
22:1–21; 26:1–29; Phil 3:5–16; 1 Tim 1:12–17). By telling
stories, the apostle communicated to others the strength and
truth of God's grace as he had experienced it personally. You
should do the same.

The Basic Groundwork

Everybody who knows and loves Christ and His Church has a story to tell, a testimony to give. To evangelize effectively you should develop a way to share your testimony and be ready, willing, and able to share it at every opportunity the Lord provides. There is spiritual power in your personal testimony because the power comes from on high (Acts 1:8). When you share God's love with someone, you act as an instrument of salvation in that person's life, and the Spirit of God truly works in and through you.

Why Share Your Personal Testimony?

Your personal testimony relates your own experience of how you came to know the Lord. This is a particularly powerful way to evangelize because nobody can argue with your own experience of how Jesus has changed your life. Your testimony narrates your relationship with Jesus Christ, Who is a Divine Person. It is Jesus you are primarily witnessing about, and it is Jesus you seek to glorify in your testimony. This is why your personal experience speaks volumes about the Gospel.

Your personal testimony is about not only the "Who" of Jesus, but also the "what" He has done in your life. Think about this for a moment. Divine intervention has happened in your life because of Jesus! How do you react to this? Are you humbled? Are you grateful? Are you excited to talk about it? I hope so, because very often people are touched precisely because you are sharing your life experiences with zeal, humility, and an attitude of gratitude.

Talking about our Lord and His Church may mean very little to someone unless you share how you have been transformed. Your testimony makes the story of salvation in the Bible and the lordship of Jesus Christ, real, specific, and personal. This is why practicing virtue and living in the presence of God are so important; it is your personal holiness that makes your testimony convincing.

Developing Your Personal Testimony

Whether you are a convert or a cradle Catholic it is vital that you find your own unique way of sharing your personal faith testimony. There are several approaches you may take. Consider these five effective "testimony types" and decide which approach will be most effective for you to communicate the love of Christ to others:

1. My personal walk with the Lord
2. The reasons I love being a Catholic
3. The Catholic Church as the Church founded by Jesus Christ
4. My conversion
5. God's call and my vocation

You may think that number four is only for converts to Catholicism from other religions or Christian denominations or that number five is just for priests and religious. But let me stress that *any* of these formats can be used by *any* Catholic, because every baptized person has a vocation and everyone has a conversion when he becomes serious in his commitment to living for Christ. That is why your personal faith witness is the most important kind of testimony.

Think about it. Why did you commit your life to Jesus?
When did you make a conscious decision to live for Him?
People will be interested. As president of Saint Joseph Communications and chairman of Lighthouse Catholic Media I
have helped to distribute widely the personal witness stories of Scott Hahn, Tim Staples, Stephen K. Ray, Matthew
Kelly, and many, many others. It is no exaggeration to
say that millions of listeners around the country and the
world have been moved by these personal stories. I know
from long experience how this kind of testimony resonates
with people. Your conversion experience can also be a
jumping-off point to other dimensions of your journey of
faith.

The five testimony types are all effective, but they are
by no means the only ways to share your personal witness.
Whichever model you choose, however, remember to keep
it simple and centered on one event. Whether your conversion was from another religion or denomination or from a
worldly life to a Christ-centered one, it is the *transformation*
—for example, from hatred to love; sadness to joy; despair
to hope; anger to happiness; weakness to strength; aimless-
ness to a sense of purpose; guilt to acceptance; bondage to
freedom; loneliness to a sense of community; or rebellious-
ness to obedience—that will appeal to people.

When you have identified the model that best fits your
personal story, it is time to arrange your testimony into three
parts:

1. Before you committed your life to the Lord
2. God's "Divine invasion" and your conversion
3. Your new life in Jesus Christ

Arranging your talk in this way gives your testimony the all-important structure of effective communication: a beginning, a middle, and an end.

1. **Before You Committed Your Life to the Lord** – *O was more of a relativist*

Your testimony will begin with some personal history: your family background and upbringing, your vocation in life, your interests, and so forth. Then you will share more specifically about your "past life", that is, the way things were before you committed yourself to Jesus Christ and His Church (cf. Acts 22:1–5; 26:4–5). Be honest about the sinful areas of your past life (cf. Acts 26:9–11). Do not romanticize or glamorize your sinful past, but make it interesting. Just be sure to exercise the virtue of prudence regarding the details. Also, a little self-deprecating humor can go a long way here.

2. **God's "Divine Invasion" and Your Conversion** – *O don't think O had a divine invasion*

The "Divine invasion" is a term coined by Venerable Fulton J. Sheen: "There are two births of Christ: one unto this world in Bethlehem, the other in the soul when it is spiritually reborn. Both result from a kind of Divine invasion." How did Christ come into your life in a personal way? How did the "Divine invasion" happen in the story of your life?

As you relate the facts of your story, be specific. Do not just say, "It happened"; rather say *what* happened. Remember, it is *your* story, but the main character is our Savior. So do not concentrate primarily on yourself, but on Jesus Christ. Emphasize the reality of Jesus in your life and your newfound relationship with Him. The key is how God

O am just struggling to be a better person & know w/ GOD in my life O am,

intervened in your life and your response to Him. The main point of your entire witness is the way you have become a "new creation" (2 Cor 5:17) in Jesus Christ—especially through His grace communicated through the sacraments —and the transformation that has come about in your life (cf. Acts 26:12–19).

3. Your New Life in Jesus Christ

Express clearly the differences in your life now that you "have the mind of Christ" (cf. 1 Cor 2:16). Your conversion experience should be compelling enough to make the person you are evangelizing want what you have: a relationship with Jesus Christ that resulted when you entered the Church or returned to the practice of the Faith.

Once again, prudence is essential. Do not exaggerate your new life in Jesus Christ. Life is still full of trials, tribulations, and sufferings. Venerable Fulton Sheen said, "Without Good Friday, there is no Easter Sunday" (cf. Rom 8:18). Rather share the benefits of having "put on Christ" (Gal 3:27, RSV), such as your new outlook on life; your ability to forgive; your new freedom, which may include freedom from addiction or bad habits but is most especially liberation from the enslavement of sin and the bondage of the devil. The key is the transformation that took place in your life because of the liberating power of Jesus Christ, which gives you a supernatural perspective on life.

Be sure to paint the picture of your real-life situation with specific, concrete examples and true stories. Ultimately, the goal is to proclaim Jesus Christ and how He is to be discovered and experienced personally through the sacraments of His Church. Your witness should gradually unveil the person of Jesus Christ, which is the climax of your testimony.

Light from the Word

"I am not ashamed of the gospel: It is the power of God for salvation to every one who has faith" (Rom 1:16, RSV).

"For the kingdom of God is not a matter of talk but of power" (1 Cor 4:20).

"Always be prepared to make a defense to any one who calls you to account for the hope that is in you, yet do it with gentleness and reverence" (1 Pet 3:15–16, RSV).

"You are our letter, written on our hearts, known and read by all, shown to be a letter of Christ administered by us, written not in ink but by the Spirit of the living God, not on tablets of stone but on tablets that are hearts of flesh" (2 Cor 3:2–3)

"But you will receive power when the holy Spirit comes upon you, and you will be my witnesses" (Acts 1:8).

Personal Testimony Dos and Don'ts

Knowing that your testimony points to eternal life and is filled with the Holy Spirit, here is a list of dos and don'ts to keep in mind when you are sharing it with others.

Dos

- Be open to the Holy Spirit's inspiration, and don't rely solely on your own human gifts.

- Speak about your personal relationship with Christ.

- Be clear about the fact that Jesus has come into your life through the Church.

- Share what the Holy Spirit is actively doing in your life through the graces you receive in the sacraments.

- Prepare a couple of stories (preferably personal) that you can use for your testimony.

- Use "word pictures" so that your testimony will paint a clear image in people's minds.

- Pray every day to strengthen your covenantal relationship with Christ and His Bride, the Church.

- Know your audience: be ready to adapt your testimony to your listener.

- Use examples from your life that relate to your listener, whether sports, travel, cars, school, and so forth.

- Speak confidently and boldly, but don't be confrontational.

- Share your testimony in an interesting way.

- Be aware that you will need to leave out many things.

- Look into the eyes of your listener, call him by name, and let him know he has your undivided attention.

- Remember that a little self-deprecating humor can relieve a tense situation.

Don'ts

- Don't come across as a know-it-all.

- Don't be long-winded: keep it brief; do not prolong your testimony with unnecessary details.

- Don't reprimand, rebuke, or speak uncharitably about others (clergy, teachers, parents, other institutions or churches, and so forth).

- Don't overemphasize the sinful or negative parts of your life. In other words, don't glamorize sin.

- Don't overuse jargon or clichés. Use your own original thoughts and words.

- Don't share your testimony without the guidance of the Holy Spirit (cf. 1 Cor 3:1).

- Don't use flowery generalities or abstractions that make it seem as if you're already in the Promised Land.

- Don't exaggerate or embellish your testimony for effect. Your truthful, simple testimony is the most effective testimony.

- Don't give away the punch line to your testimony at the beginning. Unravel your testimony slowly to the climactic point at which your audience knows that Jesus has become your Lord.

PART THREE

THE EVANGELIST'S
SPIRITUAL GAME PLAN

11

THE POWER OF PRAYER

Prayer helps us rediscover the loving face of God. He never abandons His people, but guarantees that, notwithstanding trials and sufferings, good triumphs in the end.

— Pope Blessed John Paul II

We cannot engage culture unless we let Him first engage us; we cannot dialogue with others unless we first dialogue with Him; we cannot challenge unless we first let Him challenge us. The Venerable Servant of God, Fulton J. Sheen, once commented, "The first word of Jesus in the Gospel was 'come'; the last word of Jesus was 'go'."

— Timothy Cardinal Dolan, Address to the USCCB General Assembly, 2012

I have already mentioned that a life of prayer is essential for the would-be evangelist. The liturgical prayer of the Church includes the Divine Office, also known as the Liturgy of the Hours, and, of course, the "source and summit" of the Catholic life of prayer: the Holy Mass. But in your personal prayer life there are different ways of praying and different forms of prayer. There are four basic forms:

1. Vocal Prayer

Reciting specific prayers such as the Our Father or the Hail Mary is vocal prayer. Saying the responses at Mass is also a form of vocal prayer.

2. Mental Prayer

A more advanced form, mental prayer is more like a conversation with God. It includes speaking to God and listening to Him in your heart.

3. Meditation

Christian meditation is prayerful reflection on some important truth of the Faith. You can meditate, for example, on a passage from the Bible or from another spiritual work in order to deepen your understanding of it.

4. Contemplation

In contemplation, you quiet your mind and heart and without words focus your loving attention on God, not unlike the way you would gaze into your beloved's eyes.

You should strive to practice all these forms of prayer, because in the end, prayer is not for God's benefit at all, but for ours. Through prayer we develop a relationship with God, and to be in relationship with God is what we are made for. The power of prayer can transform you into the best version of yourself—the person God wants you to be.

The Four Ends of Prayer

There are four ends, or objectives, of prayer that can be remembered by the acronym ACTS:

- Adoration
- Contrition
- Thanksgiving
- Supplication

All four objectives are present most perfectly in the Holy Mass, but they should also be present in your daily personal vocal and mental prayer.

Adoration

To adore is to worship. This first great end of prayer acknowledges who God is and praises Him for His glory.

Contrition

Through acts of contrition we express true sorrow and repentance for our sins. We acknowledge our responsibility before God for offending Him by what we have done and what we have failed to do.

Thanksgiving

As the word implies, this means thanking God for everything. It is a profound truth that every good thing we have comes from God. In fact, the only thing we can offer God that He did not first give to us is our sins, which we do give Him whenever we confess them. Cultivating an attitude of gratitude in prayer helps us to overcome envy, jealousy, and depression.

Supplication

This is what most people think of when they hear the word *prayer*: asking God for His assistance in all our needs, both spiritual and material. Jesus Himself said: "Ask and it will be given to you; seek and you will find; knock and the door will be opened to you. For everyone who asks, receives; and the one who seeks, finds; and to the one who knocks, the door will be opened" (Mt 7:7–8).

It is good to remember, however, that God answers prayers in the way that is best for us. So we should follow the example of our Lord in the Garden of Gethsemane and always pray, "Not my will but yours be done" (Lk 22:42).

As you can see, prayer is more than a mere wish list you give to God, but a genuine communication with Him. That is why we must take the next step and make our prayer a real conversation with God.

Cultivating Mental Prayer

We are contingent creatures, that is to say, we exist and have purpose only in relationship with God. Prayer brings us more deeply into that relationship; nourishes it, sustains it, and helps it grow. Catholics tend to be good at vocal prayer, and this is necessary, but to enter into a deeply personal relationship with God that empowers us to share Him with others, we must also cultivate the practice of mental prayer.

We need to communicate silently with God about what is on our minds and in our hearts. Why? Because we need to hear His voice speaking within us about the problems we face and the decisions we make in our daily lives. After all, conversation involves not only speaking, but also listening. Through the practice of resting in God's presence and opening our minds and hearts to Him we learn to listen and to receive the grace He wants to give us.

Seeking God's perspective through mental prayer will help you to understand the people you live and work with, because God's perspective teaches you to see them with His eyes. The consistent practice of mental prayer compels you to contemplate how God would have you solve a problem or resolve a difficulty, and it helps to check your own impulses to react out of anger or frustration.

Seeing with God's eyes helps you to treat others in the right way and at the right time. Because mental prayer connects you to the God of justice and mercy, a habit of mental prayer will enable you to consider what is truly just and merciful in every situation.

Practical Prayer Tips

Every time you pray, you choose God. The more often you make that choice, the easier prayer will become and the more you will find yourself praying. It is a circle of grace leading you into a deeper relationship with God in ways that you cannot foresee. Here are some practical tips to remember:

Be Aware

Before you pray, focus on the fact that God is present and listening.

Slow Down

When reading the Scriptures or other spiritual material (works of the Fathers and Doctors of the Church, lives of the saints, and so forth), allow yourself enough time to absorb the words. Don't race from passage to passage. Treat these readings like a love letter from God. Ask Him to help you understand the connections between the words on the page and the circumstances in your life.

Praise and Thank God Always

Never take God's love or goodness for granted. Praise and thank Him for all that He is and all that He has done for you.

Tell God You Are Sorry

You do not have to wait for confession to examine your conscience. Make a habit of doing this nightly. Then express your contrition and ask for the grace to do better the next day.

Listen for God's Voice

In a still, small voice God speaks to you through the movements of your soul. Cultivate an awareness of joy, sorrow, and inspirations to do good as you pray.

Plan for Prayer

Do not let a day go by without making time for God. Schedule a daily appointment with God, and never miss it. Also develop a rhythm of prayer throughout the day. Pray the Angelus at noon, say Grace before meals, and begin a difficult task with a brief invocation (e.g., "Lord, make haste to help me.").

Make Your Whole Life a Prayer

You can make your whole life a prayer by making a gift of yourself at every opportunity. Abstain from something that would give you pleasure as you pray for someone, give generously to someone in need, set aside your own plans to help another, and so forth. Every time you make one of these sacrifices—big or small—say in the silence of your heart, "Lord, I give this to You" (cf. Mt 25:40).

Light from the Word

We need to pray constantly

"Rejoice always. Pray without ceasing. In all circumstances give thanks, for this is the will of God for you in Christ Jesus" (1 Thess 5:16–18).

God answers our prayers

"Ask and it will be given to you; seek and you will find; knock and the door will be opened to you. For everyone who asks, receives; and the one who seeks, finds; and to the one who knocks, the door will be opened" (Mt 7: 7–8).

"Whatever you ask for in prayer with faith, you will receive" (Mt 21:22).

Offer God thanks and praise

"Let us come before him with a song of praise, joyfully sing out our psalms" (Ps 95:2).

"That I may praise God's name in song and glorify it with thanksgiving" (Ps 69:31).

"I give thanks to my God always on your account for the grace of God bestowed on you in Christ Jesus" (1 Cor 1:4).

Express contrition in your prayer

"My sacrifice, O God, is a contrite spirit; a contrite, humbled heart, O God, you will not scorn" (Ps 51:19).

Remember to listen

"Speak, Lord, your servant is listening" (cf. 1 Sam 3:10b).

Intercede for others in prayer

"[H]elp us with prayer, so that thanks may be given by many on our behalf for the gift granted us through the prayers of many" (2 Cor 1:11).

"The fervent prayer of a righteous person is very powerful" (James 5:16b).

God knows how best to answer our prayers

"Not my will but yours be done" (Lk 22:42).

12

WILL POWER

In *The Pope & the CEO* Andreas Widmer recounts John Paul II's explanation of what drove him to proclaim God's truth even in the face of hostile opposition:

> In 1988, shortly after the pope returned from a visit to Berlin, I was standing guard outside his private apartment when the future Pope Benedict XVI, Cardinal Joseph Ratzinger, stopped by for a visit. The Cardinal had been with the pope in Berlin, where less than friendly crowds greeted them. Activists staged huge protests, and threw eggs and tomatoes at the "popemobile" as it drove by.
>
> While Cardinal Ratzinger waited for admittance to the rooms, I began to chat with him. He's a gentle man, shy but friendly and sincere. That particular day I was curious about the reception Berlin had given the two and asked what it was like to be attacked by them. "Doesn't it bother you to have eggs and tomatoes thrown at you? Doesn't it hurt your feelings?"
>
> He smiled in his gentle way and explained, "No, because what they're throwing they're not throwing at Karol Wojtyła and Joseph Ratzinger. If the two of us had never been involved in Christ's message, they wouldn't be throwing anything at us. The tomatoes and insults are intended for what we stand for and what we proclaim. It is the Christian Faith, which has been handed down to us through the centuries. We can't change that because it is difficult to live

up to or doesn't fit the current cultural trends. We should proclaim it in love, but it is not ours to change."

How the Cardinal saw the situation was how John Paul II saw it. Christ had given them a message, the Good News. Reason had given them a framework, the person-centered ethic. They could only be truly successful if they were faithful to that; if they held true to what they had been given and upheld the ultimate dignity of the human person regardless of the cost. In their fidelity to what is right, what is true, they found their strength.

Pope John Paul II always focused on the task at hand and chose to respond in the way he believed God wanted him to respond. He was able to do this because over a period of many years, he had made a habit of choosing the right course of action. He had learned to discipline his will and to choose the good even when the choice was difficult. Simply put, he had learned to use his will rightly.

Free Will

God has given you free will, and in many ways, it is what gives your life meaning. Without free will your actions, whether good or bad, would have no significance because they would not be freely chosen. Without free will there would be no sin because sin involves knowing that an action is morally wrong but freely choosing to do it anyway. Likewise there could be no such thing as virtue because virtue requires a free choice to do what is right. It is free will that makes it possible for you to be a sinner or a saint. This is why it is crucial to train your will.

Good Will Training

Training your will to do what is right and good requires cultivating the habit of right thinking, that is, controlling the thoughts on which you allow your mind to dwell. For example, when you resent something about your life, your resentment becomes the focus of your thoughts. Every little difficulty becomes magnified. If, on the other hand, you resist thoughts that feed feelings of resentment and replace them with thoughts of gratitude for all the good things in your life, you will be willing to embrace whatever you are called upon to do. The attitude of gratitude will help you to overcome any obstacle placed in your way. What am I saying? Attitude affects your performance.

I will freely admit that cultivating the habit of controlling my thoughts is an ongoing process for me, but I continue to persevere. I do not want to allow myself to dwell on bad thoughts. When we start to entertain bad thoughts—temptations to power, greed, dishonesty, sexual immorality, drunkenness, gluttony, callousness, or other destructive behaviors—bad actions follow. All bad choices are the results of bad thoughts.

How do you overcome bad thoughts? You choose to focus on your commitment to God and family. When a bad thought enters your head, try to replace it with a good one. When you focus on good thoughts, you lay the groundwork for right action. In this way you encourage your will to move in the direction of the good and true. In effect, you nourish your will with what it needs to choose rightly.

And don't forget: you don't have to wait until a bad thought comes to focus on a good thought. In fact you can

—and should—create good thoughts. Your free will is like a muscle. It needs to be trained and strengthened in order to work properly. It needs to be disciplined. If not used well, it becomes weak. But through repeated small exercises—honoring a daily commitment to prayer, keeping promises to your spouse and children, and so on—your will to do good becomes stronger.

Practicing self-denial will also strengthen your will. Forgoing small comforts and pleasures—passing up dessert, getting up as soon as your alarm goes off, giving up TV on the weekend—are acts of sacrifice that help bring the will under the control of the intellect. The more you practice choosing what is good but difficult in small matters, the easier it will become to choose what is good but difficult in large matters.

Detaching Yourself from Pride

The great enemy of training your will is pride. Saint Augustine wrote that the three most important ingredients in living a virtuous life are humility, followed by humility, and still more humility. He also said, "At the root of vice is the opposite of humility, pride. Pride, after all, was man's original sin." Adam and Eve wanted to be like gods. They wanted to be their own God choosing for themselves what is good and what is evil. They neither trusted nor obeyed. Our culture does a fine job of imitating our first parents. And, I must admit, pride has been at the source of many struggles in my own life.

The problem many of us have is that we think we are the reason for our success. We take all the credit when things go right and start to believe our own press. We ignore the good advice of others and become self-righteous and self-centered. When we let our pride blind us to the truth about ourselves, as Adam and Eve did, we fall.

Pride is insidious because it eats away at our sense of who we really are—creatures dependent upon our Creator. The sin of pride goes to the heart of human identity and so can be found in every human endeavor, including evangelization. Pride can destroy marriages, friendships, and careers. Empires have fallen because of pride. We insist that we are right no matter how wrong we really are. We ignore wise counsel, refuse to ask for help, and lie about our weaknesses. It is pride that blinds us to the gifts that others have and are.

Humility is the virtue that opposes the vice of pride. Some people incorrectly assume that humility is thinking badly of oneself. Rather, humility involves thinking rightly of oneself. In the words of the "one-minute manager", Kenneth Blanchard, "People with humility don't think less of themselves, they think of themselves less." You overcome pride by understanding who you are and Who made you and by learning to depend on God and to obey His will. Another antidote to pride is seeing your desires as secondary and the needs of others as primary. Cultivating humility is the key to training the will. This is a simple truth, but like many simple things, it is not easy.

Training the will to choose what is right and good may seem all but impossible at first. But the more you humbly cooperate with God's grace in your life and consistently practice doing what is right, the easier it will become. That ease brings peace, joy, and the ability to do all that God has prepared for you. The more you train your will, the more you will become the best version of yourself: the person God created you to be. And this is at the very heart of evangelization.

13

THE SECRET OF EVANGELIZATION: LIVING IN THE PRESENCE OF GOD

This is without a doubt the most challenging chapter in this little book, but if you will take the time to read and to absorb it, it will bear much fruit in your life. Effective evangelization flows from your right relationship with God, and a right relationship with Him includes always living in His presence. The following chapter is adapted from the practices of the Opus Sanctorum Angelorum (Work of the Holy Angels), an international movement within the Catholic Church that is faithful to the Magisterium.

What Is Living in the Presence of God?

Living in the presence of God consists in giving loving attention—in every situation of your life—to the fact that God lives in your soul. Connected to this is the pure intention that all your words and actions correspond to the will of God and are done for His greater glory. By practicing this attention and intention, it will become a habit to live in God's presence without any special effort.

Living in the presence of God is a fruit of prayer, and it leads your soul to an ever greater union with Him. As

Jesus taught us, we need to "pray always without becoming weary" (Lk 18:1). "Pray without ceasing", echoed Saint Paul (1 Thess 5:17).

Praying constantly requires living in the presence of God and being in communion with Him. This communion of life is always possible because through baptism we have already been united with Christ. Through a constant living in the presence of God, our whole life becomes a prayer.

In this sense, you can remain recollected (aware of being in the presence of God) without going off to a quiet corner. You can form the habit of seeing Jesus in the people and circumstances of everyday life. Blessed Teresa of Calcutta said:

> [One aspect] of our life of contemplation is simplicity, which makes us see the face of God in everything, everyone, and everywhere, all the time, and His hand in all that happens; and makes us do all that we do—whether we think, study, work, speak, eat, or take our rest—under the loving gaze of the Father, being totally available to Him in any form He may come to us.

With this perspective, then, if we receive a kind word, we can say, "Thank You, Jesus!" Or if someone humiliates us, we can still say, "Thank You, Jesus!" We must treasure these gifts as coming from our Lord Himself, for "where your treasure is, there also will your heart be" (Mt 6:21). It is not necessary to do great things; just small things with great love for Jesus. As Cardinal Ratzinger (now Pope Emeritus Benedict XVI) said:

> A man open to God's presence realizes that God is always working. . . . We must therefore let Him in and let Him

work. . . . To be holy does not mean being superior to others; a saint can be very weak, with many mistakes in his life. Holiness is this profound contact with God, becoming a friend of God.

One of the five characteristics of true friendship, as explained by Saint Thomas Aquinas, is that friends take comfort in one another's company. Living in the presence of God is the beginning and the fruit of a more profound contact and friendship with God.

I must pause here to underline an important truth: Living in the presence of God is not an option for Catholic Christians! If we want to become perfect (cf. Mt 5:48), we must earnestly strive to live in the presence of God. In his *True Spouse of Jesus Christ*, Saint Alphonsus Liguori states, "The practice of the presence of God is justly called by spiritual masters the foundation of the spiritual life." You cannot build a house without a firm foundation, for it would collapse with the first storm. In the same way, you cannot live the spiritual life without striving to live in the presence of God as the foundation.

Sunlight is necessary for a plant's survival. Only under its warm and continual influence will the plant blossom and bear fruit. Just as sunlight is necessary for the full development of a plant, so living continually in the presence of God is necessary for the fruitful growth of your soul.

Many Catholics wonder why they do not advance in the spiritual life even though they pray every day or even attend daily Mass. But where are their thoughts during the rest of the day? Are they immersing themselves in worldly affairs, trying to manage them according to their natural abilities without giving any further attention to the fact that God dwells in their souls? How many more graces God would grant them—and how much more they would advance in the spiritual life—if they were really to live in the presence of God at every moment! A soul that does not strive to live every moment in the presence of God will make very slow progress in the spiritual life.

As long as a Christian does not walk in the presence of God, mere creatures—including himself—remain the center of his thoughts and desires. God, meanwhile, remains more or less on the margins. But as soon as a Christian begins to walk in the presence of God, God becomes the center. Creatures, including his own ego, fall into the background, thus leaving the road wide open to an intimate union of love with God; that is, the road to perfection. Saint Alphonsus Liguori expresses this reality when he says:

> The morning and evening meditation are not sufficient to keep the soul united to God. St. Chrysostom says that even water, if removed from the fire, soon returns to its natural temperature; therefore it is necessary to preserve fervor by practicing the presence of God and by renewing our affections.

Our Lord tells us that "the Kingdom of God is within you" (Lk 17:21b, GNT). Therefore we need to seek the Lord where He dwells, within our souls. The interior life refers to the practice of turning the attention of our mind and heart to God.

In our Lord's parable of the ten virgins (Mt 25:1–13) He says that "five of them were foolish, and five were wise." Like the wise, the foolish also wanted to meet the bridegroom, but they did not have enough oil for their lamps.

What is oil? Oil is a fuel to sustain fire. If the fuel runs out, the fire goes out. We need "oil" to keep the fire of our love for God burning. This fuel is the attentiveness we give to God dwelling in our soul. A person does this by living in the world while being "not of the world" (Jn 17:16), that is, never totally immersed in external and worldly affairs. Rather by living in the presence of God, he is able to keep and to increase the flame of love burning in his heart all through the day.

Many faithful Catholics mistakenly think that this practice is just for priests and religious or for "progressed" or "perfect" souls who are favored by mystical graces. On the contrary, as we saw above, walking in the presence of God is the *foundation* of the spiritual life; living in the presence of God is for beginners! If we want to advance significantly in the spiritual life, we must strive to live in the presence of God. By doing this we can hope to be purified from weaknesses and prevented from falling into the same sins. In the words of Saint Teresa of Avila:

> I know that, with God's help, if you practice [living in the presence of God] for a year, or perhaps for only six months, you will be successful in attaining it. Think what a short time that is for acquiring so great a benefit, for you will be laying a good foundation, so that, if the Lord desires to raise you up to achieve great things, He will find you ready, because you will be close to Him. May His majesty never allow us to withdraw ourselves from His presence. Amen.

The Effects of Living in the Presence of God

Living in the presence of God results in several beneficial effects:

- Preserves us from sin
- Increases our faith
- Strengthens our hope
- Perfects our love
- Brings us closer to our guardian angels

Preserves Us from Sin

Saint Alphonsus Liguori tells us, "There is no more efficacious means of subduing the passions, of resisting temptations, and consequently avoiding sin than by the remembrance of the presence of God." A priest heard the confession of a young boy who had stolen something. He asked the boy, "You did not steal it while anyone was watching, did you?"

"Of course not, Father!" answered the boy.

The priest replied, "But do you not know that God and your guardian angel are always watching?"

The child's eyes grew large with this new insight.

Saints who earnestly strove for sanctity would bravely reject the temptation to sin by the mere thought that God was present. Thus, in the book of Daniel we read how the thought of God's presence gave Susanna the strength to resist the unlawful advances of the elders even to the point of accepting death. She steadfastly refused to give in to their evil intentions, exclaiming, "If I yield it will be my death; if I refuse I cannot escape your power. Yet it is better for me not to do it and to fall into your power than to sin before the Lord" (Dan 13:22b–23).

I will give the last word to Saint John Chrysostom:

> If we but consider that God is everywhere present, hears all things, sees all things, not only whatsoever is done and said, but also all that is in the heart, and in the depth of the soul, for He is "quick to discern the thoughts and intentions of the heart" [cf. Heb 4:12], if we so dispose ourselves, we shall not do or say or imagine anything that is evil!

Increases Our Faith

According to Brother Lawrence, author of the seventeenth-century classic on this subject, the first benefit a person receives from practicing the presence of God is increased faith. There is a simple reason for this, Brother Lawrence explains: the more we practice being aware of God's presence in our life, the more we call out to Him and obtain from Him what we need. This becomes a virtuous cycle: being aware of God, asking for His help, experiencing His care for us, and then believing even more in His presence in our life.

As our faith in God increases, so does our ability to see beyond our failures and weaknesses and those of others. We begin to see in others the image of God and to see them as Christ's brothers and sisters, for whom He shed His Precious Blood.

As our faith increases, we also become more sensitive to the reality of sin, as something that deeply offends God and brings great damage to our souls. Finally, as we are strengthened in faith we begin to see the crosses in our lives (cf. Lk

9:23) for what they really are. Suffering in our lives is not simply something painful and frustrating, but a gift from God for our purification and sanctification and a powerful means of being even closer to Christ.

Such enlightenment of soul cannot be achieved by natural intelligence or theological study, but is a fruit of living in the presence of God.

Strengthens Our Hope

Thinking frequently about God's perfections significantly deepens our awareness that He is almighty, loving, and always faithful; He will never let us down. When we are strengthened by this awareness, we will not become discouraged or despair in trials and suffering. Rather we will trust in God's providence and courageously resign ourselves to His will.

When Empress Eudoxia threatened Saint John Chrysostom with exile, the courageous patriarch gave her an answer driven by the supernatural virtue of hope: "You would succeed in frightening me only if you could send me to a place where God is not." By that he meant that God—who is almighty and all loving—is everywhere. So wherever she might send him, God would be with him. And if God was with him, he would have nothing to fear. As Saint Paul says, "If God is for us, who can be against us?" (Rom 8:31).

Perfects Our Love

As we live in the presence of God, considering frequently His perfections—His omnipotence, wisdom, holiness, goodness, fidelity, and love—we will often be inspired to do new acts of love for God. The more frequent our acts of love, the stronger and more perfect our love for God will be "for to love is learned by loving". Just as a man cannot stand near a fire without being warmed, in the same way, when we approach God by living in His presence, we will be more and more inflamed by His love. He will strengthen us in the practice of virtue. Consider Saint Basil's rule: "Let us carry about with us the pious thought of God like an enduring mind-set! For that is the manner of prayer through which the love of God is usually attained." When you make frequent acts of love, you will have confidence that you are loved by God, as our Lord Himself promised, "Whoever loves me will be loved by my Father, and I will love Him and reveal myself to him" (Jn 14:21b).

So foster the hope that by practicing this discipline of heart, God will

> grant you in accord with the riches of his glory to be strengthened with power through his Spirit in the inner self, and that Christ may dwell in your hearts through faith; that you, rooted and grounded in love, may have strength to comprehend with all the holy ones what is the breadth and length and height and depth, and to know the love of Christ that surpasses knowledge, that you may be filled with all the fullness of God. (Eph 3:16–19)

The beatific vision in heaven consists in seeing God as He is (cf. 1 John 3:2) and in loving Him unceasingly. Happiness on our earthly pilgrimage also consists in seeing and loving God, not visibly as He is in heaven, but with the eyes of faith, through which we behold Him always present to us. As we behold Him in this way, our faith will increase, our hope will grow strong, and our love will be enkindled more and more.

Brings Us Closer to Our Guardian Angels

In our spiritual struggle to live in God's presence, we must make an effort to know and to reverence God with our whole being, seeking His will in all that we do. In this way we will also draw nearer to the holy angels, learn to understand them, and imitate their fidelity, humility, and readiness to serve. This state of recollection—the foundation of the spiritual life—is also the habitual state of contact (i.e., conversation) with our guardian angels. By living always in the presence of God, we begin, even in this "valley of tears", to live like angels who "always look upon the face of [our] heavenly Father" (Mt 18:10).

The lives of the saints teach us that souls who persevere through "dry" periods in their spiritual life will, by the grace of God, achieve union with Him. No one achieves this by his own efforts alone, nor does anyone achieve the state of recollection without being ready to start over a thousand times a day. And your guardian angel is ready to help you in this. He can lead you along the path of recollection. When you fall, he is there to pick you up and encourage you to start again. He will help you to see through the situations of daily life to God, who stands behind all things.

So what are you waiting for? Start today on this path of loving attention to the presence of God with courage and zeal, in the company of your guardian angel. I pray that through this spiritual exercise and with the help of your guardian angel you will experience God's warmth and nearness as you reach out to Him in prayer and become ever more conscious of His loving presence.

14

YOUR SPIRITUAL GAME PLAN

Do you want to be an effective evangelist? Then you must be a good Christian. To be a good Catholic Christian it is of first importance to love God above all things, to avoid mortal sin, and to remain in a state of grace. This way of living in the presence of God will also help you to avoid committing even venial sins.

To live in the presence of God even in the midst of your busy daily routine requires making regular acts of piety a part of that routine. Making a habit of such acts is your foundation for growing in virtue. Sticking to this "spiritual game plan" will help you live as a true child of God:

Daily Exercises

The following daily exercises make a good spiritual game plan.

Rise at a Fixed Time

Get up as early as possible, but be sure to get enough sleep. Eight hours of sleep should be enough. As a general rule, more than eight or less than seven hours of sleep is unhealthful.

Make a Morning Offering

Offer your day to God through the intercession of Mary.

A prayer for making a morning offering is in the Favorite Prayers section in the back of this book.

Try to Attend Holy Mass

Go to Mass and receive Communion as often as possible. We are closest to God when we receive Him in Holy Communion. When we allow enough time to pray before Mass begins, we are better recollected and less distracted during Mass.

Spend Time in Mental Prayer

About fifteen minutes is good. If possible make this exercise before the Blessed Sacrament. Mental prayer can also follow reading the Scriptures or other spiritual material. When a person is not able to attend Mass, reading the Scripture verses chosen for that day's Mass, followed by mental prayer, can help set his day on solid footing.

Pray the Angelus

This prayer, which includes three Hail Marys followed by a prayer to God for grace, is traditionally said at six in the morning, at noon, and at six in the evening. Say it daily at least at noon to help you refocus on the Lord. During the Easter season the Regina Coeli is prayed in place of the Angelus.

Pray the Rosary

Pray five decades of the Rosary each day—if possible with your family—with a specific intention for each decade.

Spiritual Reading

Begin with the New Testament. The Church grants a partial indulgence for contemplative reading of Scripture for fifteen minutes. After the Bible, there are many excellent choices for spiritual reading. Some of my favorites are lives of the saints, *The Imitation of Christ*, *Introduction to the Devout Life*, and *The Soul of the Apostolate*.

Examine Your Conscience

Make an examination of conscience at the end of the day. Humble yourself in the presence of God, and ask the Holy Spirit to help you acknowledge your defects and virtues and to recall the opportunities and dangers of the day. Be sincerely sorry for your faults, thank God for His graces, and ask for His help and encouragement.

Weekly Exercises

Honor the Lord's Day

Sunday is the Lord's Day, a day of physical rest and spiritual growth. It is also a family day. Center the day on Holy Mass and then avoid unnecessary work so as to enjoy recreational activities with family members.

Receive Holy Communion

If you cannot receive Communion daily, receive at least on Sundays and holy days of obligation. Be sure to receive Communion worthily.

Do Penance on Friday

Because the Lord died on Good Friday, the Church has always required the faithful to do some kind of penance on Fridays. Traditionally, the Church asked Catholics to abstain from meat on Fridays, but that is no longer required, except on the Fridays during Lent. Some Catholics continue to abstain from meat on all the Fridays of the year, but there are other little sacrifices that can be made instead, such as praying the Stations of the Cross, giving to the needy, or foregoing dessert.

Honor Mary on Saturday

Saturday is traditionally dedicated to the Blessed Virgin Mary. Make sure to honor her in some special way—through the First Saturday devotion, Marian prayers such as the Hail, Holy Queen, and so forth.

Monthly Exercises

Go to Confession

Pope John Paul II said, "God is always the one who is principally offended by sin and God alone can forgive." He does this through the ministry of His priests. Pope Benedict XVI recommended that Catholics make a good confession each month.

Seek Spiritual Direction

One of the best ways to grow in the spiritual life is to seek and to follow the spiritual guidance of a wise, prudent, and knowledgeable priest.

Spend a Few Hours in Recollection

This may happen only a few minutes at a time, but if done regularly it will add up. Bishop Sheen recommended making a daily Holy Hour before the Blessed Sacrament. Put yourself in the presence of God, and consider how you are directing your life toward Him.

Yearly Exercise

Make a Retreat

In the same way that a yearly vacation is necessary for your body, a retreat of a few days—or even a week—each year is necessary for your soul. A yearly retreat spent in silence—talking only to God—is a powerful means of conversion.

Continual Exercises

Live in the Presence of God

Always be aware that God is close to you. Try always to please Him in everything, as a child tries to please a loving father.

Be Grateful

Have an attitude of gratitude. Thank God constantly for all the graces He gives to you. Thank the people around you who do things for you. God sends his blessings through the mediation of other people.

Do All for the Love of God

When the love of God is our reason for doing something, this is called having "purity of intention". Whenever you fall, make an immediate act of contrition and make atonement for your sins and those of others.

Keep the End in View

It is a simple but profound truth that you will die as you have lived. Keep this truth before you always and try to live as you would like to die. Meditate often on the four last things: death, judgment, heaven, and hell.

15

EVANGELIZATION "IN THE MARGINS"

As we near the end of this little book, I realize that everything I have shared may seem a bit overwhelming. But it does not have to be. Evangelization is the work of a lifetime, and life is lived one minute at a time. Living a life of evangelization does not mean that each day will be filled with great deeds or that you will always get immediate or even visible results. At the end of the day there will always be margins and pieces left over; but these "leftovers" are often more valuable than we realize. Every activity, however ordinary—to overcome one little temptation, to make some small sacrifice, to do one little kindness, to take a stand for God even when it seems as if it won't make a difference—is a work of grace for one who is in the state of grace.

This chapter is a collection of stories about what God can accomplish "in the margins".

A Long Drive

Going to conferences out of state is always a bit of a sacrifice for me, because I do not like to be away from my family. I recall a trip to a parish event in Arizona that was a bit more of a sacrifice than usual, as I had gone by car instead of flying. It made for an extra-long trip, what with driving there and spending all weekend at the CD table only to face the drive back home again. On top of this, the response was nothing to write home about. But I was content to do my part to promote the Faith at this little conference.

Near the end of the event a woman came up and said to me, "My daughter tried to commit suicide last week. Do you have anything here that can help us?"

I said, "Yes. I have one last copy of *10 Steps to Overcoming Depression* by Alicia Leyva, a Catholic marriage and family therapist."

As she took the set she gave me a hug and began to cry in a mixture of relief and gratitude. It was then that I realized what my little sacrifice was really for.

"You know," I told the woman, "God loves you and your daughter so much that He had a knucklehead like me drive a thousand miles just so I could hand you those CDs."

This was a time that a little sacrifice yielded a quick and visible result. Sometimes it's not so obvious.

Going against the Flow

When I was nineteen a woman from our parish confided to my dad that her husband was having an affair. Our family had known the couple for thirty years. It was a shocking revelation, but not as surprising as the fact that her husband's mistress was another fellow parishioner—and not just a fellow parishioner, but a daily communicant with whom my dad was accustomed to chat after daily Mass. My dad determined to confront the lady about the situation.

Now, I believe most people would have kept quiet for fear of offending the lady, but to "admonish the sinner" is one of the Spiritual Works of Mercy. And, as Father Bill Casey, CPM, has often said, "To leave someone in their sins is the most merciless thing I can think of." So after Mass the next day my dad politely but firmly told the woman that she was committing a serious sin that deeply offended God. He reminded her that such a sin could send her soul to hell—and the adulterous husband's soul as well—and on top of that, it was also a mortal sin of sacrilege for her to receive Holy Communion in such a state.

I am sorry to say that the lady did not accept my dad's admonition in the spirit in which it was offered. In fact, her pride was so affronted by his frankness that she said, "I will never come back to this church again, because you have offended me." And she never did. My dad took some heat over this, especially from another parishioner who blamed him for "driving her away". This, of course, is the fear that many have about confronting someone over sin: that the person will be offended and that they themselves will be blamed for making matters worse. But although my dad suffered for it, he never lost his conviction that he had done the right thing.

Unfortunately, the affair continued. Sometime later we learned that the adulterous couple was on a plane together to share a romantic getaway when the man was seized with a fatal heart attack. Although we must not judge the state of anyone's soul, it appears that this story has the most unhappy of endings.

So why do I include this story in this book? I share this episode with you because of the effect it had on me. It was a powerful illustration that our actions have real consequences, both in time and in eternity. Because of this experience I determined to be a Catholic father who would lead by example as my dad did. Even if I had to stand alone, I decided, I would gladly go against the flow any time the honor of God, the good of my soul or the good of my neighbor's soul required it. As Bishop Sheen said, "It takes fortitude to swim against the current, but even a dead body can float downstream." In the words of Pope Benedict XVI:

> Believing in God makes us carriers of values which often do not coincide with the prevailing fashion and opinion; it requires us to adopt criteria and conduct which do not belong to the common way of thinking. The Christian should not be afraid to "go against the grain" to live his or her faith. (Wednesday Audience, January 23, 2013)

Sometimes standing up for the truth has a price. The only question is, "Are we willing to pay it?"

A Row at a Rosary

Saint Joseph Communications is headquartered at Sacred Heart Chapel in Covina, California. Sacred Heart is privately owned but available for weddings, funerals, and the like. A family friend once asked to have a Rosary service there for the repose of the soul of his departed mother. A Catholic deacon was engaged to conduct the service, and I was happy to oblige, as the family could not afford a mortuary service or a big funeral.

When the evening came I asked the family about the schedule for the Rosary, and they informed me that the deacon had to cancel at the last minute. They asked if I would be able to lead the Rosary and say a few words. I agreed to stand in and mentally prepared some remarks.

There were about 120 people there for the service. After I led the Rosary, I decided to give a brief reflection on the four last things—death, judgment, heaven, and hell—as is customary at Catholic funerals. It was just a meat-and-potatoes presentation of basic catechesis, but as I gave the reflection I could see people shaking their heads at what I was saying. When I finished, I announced that we would take a short break and then family and friends could come up and share about "Grandma".

Even though things were a little tense, I thought the cordial thing to do was stand outside and give the people my condolences. As some of the younger men came outside one guy took the opportunity to chew me out with some of the foulest language I had ever heard. Furthermore, he told me, he was going to kick my you-know-what! Just as he was about to throw the first punch, an older family member stepped in his way and told him, "You are embarrassing the family! Go wait in the car."

They apologized to me, but I said, "It's no problem; I understand this is a very stressful time."

After the service I stayed behind to lock up the chapel. It was now dark. In the parking lot, who do you suppose was leaning against my car with his hands folded across his chest as if he had something to say to me? "Well," I thought, "this guy's probably looking for round two!"

When I got within about twenty feet of him I asked, "What's up?"

I was ready for a confrontation, but instead he said to me, "I just wanted to apologize for the way I acted before. Will you please forgive me?" He put his hand out to shake mine.

You can imagine my relief as I took his hand and replied, "Absolutely."

Although I was prepared to defend myself, I did not come at him with harsh words or a desire to retaliate for what he had done earlier. I tried to follow the words of Saint Peter:

> [S]anctify Christ as Lord in your hearts. Always be ready to give an explanation to anyone who asks you for a reason for your hope, but do it with gentleness and reverence, keeping your conscience clear, so that, when you are maligned, those who defame your good conduct in Christ may themselves be put to shame. (1 Pet 3:15–16)

I was ready to explain and defend the remarks I made about the four last things, but I approached this young man with the love of Christ in my heart. Of course I was both relieved and more than happy to offer genuine forgiveness in return for his sincere apology. The mourners' general reaction to the Church's teaching on the four last things, however, reveals once again how it often happens that people—even fellow Catholics—do not always appreciate it when we stand up for the truth.

A Walk Is Worth a Thousand Words

On a more joyful note, we can often reap positive results in the margins when we do not even intend to evangelize. During the first twenty years of our marriage, on most evenings Mary Danielle and I shared an arm-in-arm walk through our neighborhood, just the two of us. One evening a lady in the neighborhood said, "What's your secret?" I asked her to explain and she said, "For twenty years I've seen you two walking down the street together like you were walking down the aisle; you look like you're still really in love all these years later! So, what's your secret?"

I did not want to go into a long explanation of how love is not just an emotion, but an act of the will, so I simply told her, "It is one thing to fall in love, but that feeling doesn't last. Our love is strong because we have the power to renew it. Choosing to renew our love for one another daily is how we stay in love." She said she had never heard of such a thing before. And we got the chance to share it with her only because of our evening walks.

Another time when we were walking, a couple we had never met called to us from their front yard. "We just lost our dad", they told us when we stopped. "We see you in church on Sundays, and we can tell you really believe. Will you pray for our dad?" They did not know who else to ask.

We prayed with them for their dad's soul right then and there. God used us as a means of comfort for this couple who had lost their elderly dad, and his soul no doubt benefited from prayers that would not have been offered otherwise. But we cannot take the credit for this moment of grace. It is not just because Danielle and I take an evening walk or try to be reverent in church. Rather it came about because God chose to honor our commitment to each other and to Him in order to make use of an example we did not even realize we were setting.

A Life Saved by a Good Habit

I suppose we typically do not think of the way we behave in church as a means of evangelizing. After all, at Mass we are surrounded by fellow Catholics! But God can use the everyday aspects of our Catholic life for His purpose even when we are not doing anything extraordinary; just being faithful and devoting ourselves to good habits.

For example, a lady once approached me at a conference and said, "You probably don't remember me", and she was right: I didn't. It turns out she had been in a youth group at Saint Christopher Catholic Church in West Covina when I was a youth leader teaching catechism many years ago.

"I stopped attending the class when I got pregnant out of wedlock", she said. "My boyfriend was pressuring me to have an abortion, and I was very scared and confused. I felt like I had no one to turn to, so I went to church to pray for guidance. A few minutes after I arrived, you came in for your Holy Hour. The minute I saw you I remembered what you taught us at our youth meetings about the sanctity of life. And I became convinced not to abort my baby. Terry, I'd like you to meet my daughter." She then called a young woman over to us and said: "Mary, I want you to meet the man who kept me from aborting you." Then this young woman gave me a hug of gratitude. "Terry," the woman said, "I'm glad I finally got the chance to thank you."

"You're welcome," I said, "but any good that we do comes from God, and we thank *Him* for it." Once again, I did nothing out of the ordinary. It was God who employed a part of my regular day (Holy Hour) for His good purpose. Obviously there was no thought on my part of setting an example in a situation I did not even know about!

The Right Soul in the Wrong Place

In 1986 my father, Harry, had to undergo brain surgery after a shunt procedure. During his recuperation at the Long

Beach VA hospital, because of his delicate status, he was allowed only one visitor for five minutes every hour.

When it was my turn, an RN at the nurse's station pointed me toward my father's room, and off I went. I found him lying in bed with a sheet up to his neck, his face swollen, and so many tubes coming out of his mouth and nose that I could hardly see his shaved head. He was such a pitiful sight that I scarcely recognized him.

Sitting by his bed, I spoke to him softly about redemptive suffering, reminding him of the rewards he could expect and how his suffering would not go to waste. My five minutes nearly up, I took his hand and said, "Dad, if you heard what I said, please squeeze my hand so I'll know."

I felt his hand squeeze mine ever so gently and was blessed to know that he had understood my every word. I whispered goodbye and left the room.

As I stepped into the hallway the nurse saw me and said, "What were you doing in there?"

I said, "Visiting my dad."

She looked right at me, pointed to another room, and said, "Your father is in *that* room."

To this day I do not know who the man was that I spoke to or what became of him. But one thing I know for sure: it was God's plan to have me there to speak to him and to pray for his soul.

Divine Time Management

The one thing all these little stories have in common is the plain fact that ultimately evangelization is in the hands of

God. As I have said before, our efforts are often the least effective when we think we are doing well—scoring "points" in an argument or feeling good about ourselves. And just as often it is when we think we have accomplished the least that God does the most. As Bishop Sheen said, "God often chooses weak instruments in order that His power might be manifested. Otherwise it would seem that the good was done by the clay, rather than by the Spirit."

Each of us has his own unique gifts and talents, which have their source in God, and God wants us to use these gifts for His greater honor and glory and to expand His kingdom on earth—each according to his ability. But while there are many gifts and each of us is unique, there is one gift in which we all have a precisely equal share: time.

Every one of us has exactly the same twenty-four hours given to us each day. Young or old, rich or poor, influential or insignificant, we live each day one minute at a time. Our twenty-four-hour day is made up of 1,440 minutes, and each one is precious.

Not every day can be filled with great deeds, but we are accountable for each minute that we live. So if we cannot devote each minute to great deeds, let us at least be sure that all our time is spent in activities that are innocent and lawful. For as we have seen, even in those moments when we do not realize or intend it, God can use our time for His good purpose—if we are faithful to Him.

Light from the Word

Make good use of your time

"When you are with unbelievers, always make good use of the time. Be pleasant and hold their interest when you speak the message. Choose your words carefully and be ready to give answers to anyone who asks questions" (Col 4:5, CEV).

"Act like people with good sense and not like fools. These are evil times, so make every minute count" (Eph 5:15–16, CEV).

God is in charge of time

"It is not for you to know the times or seasons that the Father has established by his own authority. But you will receive power when the holy Spirit comes upon you, and you will be my witnesses in Jerusalem, throughout Judea and Samaria, and to the ends of the earth" (Acts 1:7–8).

"Teach us to count our days aright, that we may gain wisdom of heart" (Ps 90:12).

"But do not ignore this one fact, beloved, that with the Lord one day is like a thousand years and a thousand years is like one day" (2 Pet 3:8).

God's greatest gift came in time

"But when the fullness of time had come, God sent his Son, born of a woman" (Gal 4:4).

FAVORITE PRAYERS AND REFLECTIONS

The greatest untapped reservoir of spiritual power
is to be found in the Christian laity.

—Venerable Fulton J. Sheen

To close this little book, I want to share some prayers and useful admonitions that you may not find in a typical prayer book. Some are older, some are newer, one has been "adapted for Catholic use", but all have been an inspiration to me personally. I hope you find something here that will encourage you in your own mission of evangelization.

A Morning Offering

O, Jesus, through the Immaculate Heart of Mary,
I offer You all of my prayers, works, joys, and
    sufferings of this day,
in union with the Holy Sacrifice of the Mass
    throughout the world,
for all of the causes you have at heart,
in reparation for my sins,
for the salvation of souls,
and for the intentions of the Holy Father. Amen.

Eternal Life

Life is short and death is sure,
The hour of death remains obscure.

A soul you have and only one,
if that be lost all hope is gone.
Waste not time while time shall last,
for after death 'tis ever past.
All-seeing God your Judge will be,
and heaven or hell your destiny.
All earthly things will pass away.
Eternity alone will stay.

Surprise in Heaven

"It is very likely that there will be many surprises in heaven. Many people will be there that we never expected to find, and many will not be there whom we expected to see; and finally, we probably will be most surprised to find ourselves there." (Venerable Fulton J. Sheen, *The Quotable Fulton Sheen*)

The Spiritual Warrior's Creed
(Adapted from "A Soldier's Creed")

I am a "Soldier of God".
I am a spiritual warrior and a member of "Team Jesus".
I serve the people of God and live the Christian virtues
  and values.
I shall always place the mission first.
I shall never quit. Surrender is not an option.
I shall never leave a fallen Catholic comrade.
I am disciplined.
I am physically, mentally, morally, and spiritually tough.
I am trained and proficient in my spiritual warrior tasks
  and skills.
I always maintain my spiritual weapons, my
  equipment, and myself.

I am expert in the sure knowledge and practice of
my Catholic Faith.
I stand ready to deploy, engage, and destroy the
enemies of God and of souls in close and
immortal combat.
I am a guardian of the glorious freedom of the
children of God and the Christian way of life.

Men of Integrity—Soldiers in the Bible

"The greatest tribute that can be paid to soldiers is to recall that they are always well spoken of in Scripture. Great
soldiers are praised—such as Joshua, David, and Gideon in
the Old Testament. In the New Testament, whenever an individual soldier is mentioned he is the object of veneration
and respect. The four Roman soldiers who are mentioned in
the New Testament are men of great integrity." (Venerable
Fulton J. Sheen, *The Quotable Fulton Sheen*)

A Prayer to the Holy Spirit

Come, Holy Spirit: fill my heart with Your holy gifts.

Let my weakness be penetrated with Your strength this
very day that I may fulfill the duties of my state in life con-
scientiously, that I may do what is right and just.

Let my charity be such as to offend no one and hurt no
one's feelings; so generous as to pardon sincerely any wrong
done to me.

Assist me in all the trials of life, enlighten me in my ig-
norance, advise me in my doubts, strengthen my weakness,
help me in all needs and embarrassment, protect me in temptations, and console me in all afflictions.

Graciously hear me, O Holy Spirit, and pour Your light
into my heart, my soul, and my mind. Assist me to live a
holy life and to grow in goodness and grace. Amen.

Great Need

"Our time stands in great need of men and women who can communicate the fascination of the Gospel and the beauty of new life in the Spirit. . . . Let us implore and welcome the gift of the Holy Spirit, the light of truth, the power of authentic peace." (Pope John Paul II, "Message to Renewal in the Spirit", 2004)

Prayer to the Risen Christ
(From the *Liturgy of the Hours*)

Heavenly Father and God of mercy,
we no longer look
for Jesus among the dead,
for He is alive
and has become the Lord of life.
From the waters of death
You raise us with Him
and renew Your gift of life within us.
Increase in our minds and hearts
the risen life
we share with Christ
and help us to grow as Your people
toward the fullness of eternal life with You.
We ask this through Christ our Lord.
Amen.

Easter Joy

"Knowing that Christ is alive should fill us with joy. Knowing that He is victorious over death should inspire us to imitate Him, to live the life that He lives. It should make us want to run off and tell others about Him." (Archbishop José Gomez, "Our Joy in Easter")

A Prayer to the Holy Family for a Happy Death

Jesus, Mary, and Joseph, I give you my heart and my soul.
Jesus, Mary, and Joseph, assist me in my last agony.
Jesus, Mary, and Joseph, may I breathe forth my soul
into your blessed company.
Amen.

What Will You Take?

"There comes a time in the life of every man when at the supreme and tragic hour of death his friends and relatives ask, 'How much did he leave?' It is just at that split second God is asking, 'How much did he take with him?' It is only the latter question that matters, for it is only our works that follow us." (Venerable Fulton J. Sheen, *The Quotable Fulton Sheen*)

A Prayer to the Heart of Jesus, Mary, and Joseph

Heart of Jesus, I adore Thee,
Heart of Mary, I implore thee,
Heart of Joseph, ever just,
In this heart I place my trust.
Amen.

I especially love this last little prayer. Notice that it says "heart", not "hearts". This is because Jesus, Mary, and Joseph were perfectly united in their love for each other and their union with God. The Holy Family was the most perfect earthly expression of the Holy Trinity, so we can truly say their hearts "beat as one".

A Final Prayer

My final prayer is for you. I pray that this little book will help you to deepen your love for Christ and His Holy Church.

I pray that it will inspire you to share the Faith with others and provide the means for you to evangelize more effectively than ever before. In closing let me share with you the words of Pope Benedict XVI: "There is nothing more beautiful than to be surprised by the Gospel, by the encounter with Christ. There is nothing more beautiful than to know Him and to speak to others of our friendship with Him."

Thank you for reading this book, and may God bless you and your family.

BIBLIOGRAPHY

Catechism of the Catholic Church. New York, N.Y.: Random House/Doubleday, 1992.

Christian Prayer: Liturgy of the Hours. Totowa, N.J.: Catholic Book Publishing, 1976.

Dolan, Cardinal Timothy. Address to the USCCB General Assembly, 2012.

Gomez, Archbishop José H. "Our Joy in Easter". *Tidings*, April 6, 2012.

———. "You Will Be My Witnesses: A Pastoral Letter to the People of God of San Antonio on the Christian Mission to Evangelize and Proclaim Jesus Christ". San Antonio: Archdiocese of San Antonio, 2012.

Hahn, Scott W. *Rome Sweet Home.* San Francisco: Ignatius Press, 1993.

John Paul II. "Message for World Communications Day". Vatican City: Libreria Editrice Vaticana, 2000.

———. "Message to Renewal in the Spirit". Vatican City: Libreria Editrice Vaticana, 2004.

Lovasik, Father Lawrence J. *The Hidden Power of Kindness.* Manchester, N.H.: Sophia Institute Press, 1999.

Opus Sanctorum Angelorum. *Spiritual Formation Newsletter.* Detroit: Opus Sanctorum Angelorum, 2010.

Paul VI. *On Evangelization in the Modern World*. New York, N.Y.: United States Conference of Catholic Bishops, 1976.

Roman Missal. Huntington, Ind.: Our Sunday Visitor, 2004.

Sheen, Archbishop Fulton J. *The Quotable Fulton Sheen*. Anderson, S.C.: Droke House, 1967.

Tabers, Joseph M. *God Has a Great Plan for You*. Detroit: Discovery Learning, Inc., 2010.

Vatican II. *Decree on the Apostolate of Lay People*. Collegeville, Minn.: Liturgical Press, 1965.

———. *Decree on the Missionary Activity of the Church*. Collegeville, Minn.: Liturgical Press, 1965.

Widmer, Andreas, and George Weigel. *The Pope & the CEO: John Paul II's Leadership Lessons to a Young Swiss Guard*. Steubenville, Ohio: Emmaus Road Publishing, 2011.